MINE YOUR BUSINESS

SECOND EDITION

Keith Seville

**Grosvenor House
Publishing Limited**

This book is published by
Grosvenor House Publishing Ltd
Link House
140 The Broadway, Tolworth, Surrey, KT6 7HT.
www.grosvenorhousepublishing.co.uk

A CIP record for this book
is available from the British Library

ISBN 978-1-83975-147-9

The information contained in this book is intended solely to
provide general guidance of matters of interest for the
personal use of the reader.

Book Reviews

The thing that came across to me was not any one chapter or section but the feeling that the book was trying to install in people, which is enthusiasm, focus and to never assume that things happen by luck, although often luck plays a part.

Angela Bascombe-McCarthy, Consultant, Energy, Financial Services

This book is basically a self-empowerment autobiography taking you from humble working-class beginnings to a self-made and empowered entrepreneur. It inadvertently covers the psychology of self-belief, self-awareness laws of attraction, morals and ethics. Any budding entrepreneurs will be able to identify the deeper messages of this book.

Tim Regisford, Senior Health Care Worker

Reading this book gave me great inspiration to write my own book. This book showed me the struggles that Keith Seville had throughout his life to become a successful businessperson.

Francine Griffith, SEN Teacher

I can relate to what Keith Seville says, like being unemployable, and you needed to get out of the rat race to find your potential. Like myself I have been through a lot of jobs, so I am on my journey right now to become more successful in all areas of my life, especially as I run my own business.

Royston Denny, Self Employed Plasterer

The book is packed full of content, each page is like a day in the life of a serial entrepreneur. As a reader you are taken on a journey through the do's and don'ts of business management. The author doesn't preach about how successful each business venture was or boast about the way he did things it is rather a very realistic take on small businesses especially for those whom some deem to be "unemployable".

Dev-Anandi Rooney, Personal Trainer

'Mine Your Business is a wonderful book and will be extremely insightful to those starting or are early on in their journey down the road to self-employment. Keith does a brilliant job at showing the pitfalls in being employed and illustrates from a very personal perspective the costs but most of all the benefits of running your own business.

There are numerous nuggets of golden information contained in the book, each of Keith's personal anecdotes within the book act as strong metaphors for the budding entrepreneur who choose to take on-board the key messages.'

Derek Duncan, Director of Training

'A very easy read. Keith has outlined his philosophy on how to achieve success. From humble beginnings he has persevered against the odds to run various businesses by following his instinct. He has not allowed bureaucracy to stand in his way. It is not a book that gives you any legal advice but is based on his personal life.'

Anand Seegobin, Lecturer

'Keith your book gathered pace as it went along then I couldn't put it down as it went towards the end, would like to read another book by you giving more in depth details.'

Michael Batten, Businessman

'After struggling to get my 8-year-old daughter to read, I was pleasantly surprised to see her pick up this book and read with such interest and enthusiasm. Great inspiration for the younger generation!'

Alexandra Oyebade, Administrator

'Mine Your Business is an entertaining and perceptive journey from a first-time author detailing the highs and lows on becoming self-employed. This book is an excellent resource for anyone wanting to become self-employed, or are already on the road to becoming self-employed, but are struggling to manage the obstacles. The author provides a first-hand account of how it was possible for him to reach where he is today. The tone of the book reflects an appreciation of a remarkable journey and a desire to share this with others.'

Jackie Daniel, Senior Social Worker

'I read the book from cover to cover and from the first word I was hooked.

What I like most was the insights illustrating his personal experiences good/bad – he highlights his successes and chronicles his learning when things don't go quite to plan.

I loved the book and when I finished the final line, I knew it to have been an uplifting and inspirational experience. I began to think and wonder – is going into business possible for me and if so what would my niche be?

I cannot express my critique loudly enough: I want to know more...'

Janet Gayle-Scarlett, Senior Local Government Officer

I have read the above book you have written; I must say that it is a rather well produced book.

The people you met at your school, studying, work, friends, and family helped to make it an excellent book.

Good Luck!

Patricia Cutting, Retired

'Mine Your Business is a book that takes you on a journey of entrepreneurialism. It's an easy to follow jargon free story/account of a local man's drive to be his own boss across a number of unrelated businesses.'

Melvina Dimmott-Franklin, Accountant

'Mine Your Business' is an inspirational account of a serial entrepreneur and gives insight into how to survive in business without the backing of huge banking institutions and multi-national corporations.

I am glad I did not have to read a business manual with all its awful jargon, and I recommend it to anyone thinking of starting out in business, from the young person who is finding it difficult to hold down a job and believes they can do better, to people who have been in business to enable them to reflect and perhaps do things differently.'

Victor Koroma, General Manager

Mine Your Business inspired me on many different levels. I learnt more about my grandparents. I had no idea that my grandmother was a nurse back in the 60's or that my grandfather worked as a painter and decorator. For me, the book was more than a great read it gave me an insight of what my family's life was like before my time.

Uncle Keith's journey to self-employment was interesting. He makes it look easy, so I had no idea of what he has overcome until now. The last part of the book was a tough read for me, Our Monica. That part cut deep, as a family we all lived through that tough time. That part was also inspiring to me, Where Aunty says - Whatever plans you all have, take it from me, just do it, because you don't know what's around the corner, there is no warning. This gave me a buzz to keep on, keeping on.

Jannine Johnson, Personal Banking Manager

Contents

All that Glitters is not Gold   xi
Dedication   xiii
Acknowledgement   xv
Preface   xvii
Introduction   xix

1   Leadership   1
2   Problem Child   7
3   Your Mindset   13
4   And the Winner is...   19
5   Frogs and Trogs   27
6   Urban Warrior   33
7   Job to Job   41
8   From Mars to Benefits   47
9   Unemployable   53
10   Contact Sports   59
11   Employing Yourself   67
12   Kensington and Maidenhead   73
13   Seville Lodge   79
14   Mentee to Mentor   85
15   Capital Direct   91
16   Train the Trainer   97
17   Urban News   103

18	The Big Debate	109
19	Nesta Care	115
20	Avoiding Naysayers	121
21	Market Research	127
22	Mission Statement	133
23	Minority Mentality	139
24	Business Location	145
25	Starting Up	151
26	Marketing/Communication	157
27	Snakes and Ladders	163
28	Pricing	169
29	Getting Paid	177
30	Don't Blame the Fridge	183
31	Continued Learning	189
32	Know What You Don't Know	195
33	Managing People	201
34	Social Media	207
35	Next Step	213
36	No man is an Island	219
37	MAPP Centre	225
38	Lemon Hall	231
	Synopsis	237
	Postscript	245
	Q and A	249
	Our Monica	255
	About the Author	261
	Hall of Cards	264

'All that glitters is not gold'*

This statement shows that not everything that looks precious or true turns out to be so. This can be applied to just about any experience in life.

* Derived from a 16th-century line by William Shakespeare

Dedication

I dedicate this book to my late sister Monica Seville who was aware that I was writing a book, however she lost her fight against Motor Neurone Disease in October 2016, before the book was completed.

My family has set up an organisation in her memory called 'Our Monica'.

www.ourmonica.org.uk.

Acknowledgement

I would like to thank my mother for being an inspiration and so forthright, and for showing such leadership in our family, and to my late father for always being there when I needed him, he was a fabulous role model. To my sisters, and brother, for their continuous support, and for accepting me for who I am, complete with all my aspirations and flaws.

To Timmy, Alfred and Andrew for showing me what true friendship was especially at such a young age whilst still at school. For also making me competitive so that I could take that competitiveness into the adult world and use it to my advantage when things were stacked against me.

To my wife Nissa, for not only being patient, but helping me through the process, sometimes with the typing and proofreading well into the night. To my daughters Antonella, Iman, and Amira, for putting up with me continually going on about the book, and for helping me with their ideas and opinions. To my son Omar, for inspiring me with his unique ability to keep smiling, regardless of what life throws at him.

To my office staff Shanice Medford, Alex Oyebade, Alex Gittens, Sav Mahmood, Saqlain Jones, Zarqa

Qureshi, and my nieces Vicky Prince, and Hafsah Sofya, for their help with typing and reading parts of the transcripts, and our discussions about the book.

Finally, a big thank you to my editor, Shirley Anstis, who painstakingly trawled through each page of my transcript with such patience. Also, my business associates, voluntary community sector colleagues, staff, family, and friends to whom I owe a great deal of gratitude.

Keith Seville

Preface

This book came about through my direct experience of being an entrepreneur and wanting to share my journey with others. Like running a marathon, it takes you through the ups and downs that I have faced whilst being an entrepreneur over the years.

It has been two years since 'Mine Your Business' was first published. I had been meaning to write a book for many years and it was only when the opportunity arose, when some of the staff that work for one of my company's had some downtime, that I was able to ask them to help me to put my book together.

Many of my colleagues, whether in business, the community, or family members have said they would love to write a book however it seems that although people make such statements there are few within my circles that have achieved such.

I was very touched to have the Mayor of Reading, the Right Worshipful Cllr. Rose Williams in attendance at the launch of 'Mine Your Business' to address the crowd, at a prestigious hotel in my home county, of Berkshire in England.

There was a large turnout from the community at the launch and as a first-time author I was most humbled by their presence.

I hope that the amendments that have been made to the second edition can help to build on the success of the original book.

The original edition of Mine Your Business was successful, and I thank everyone who helped to make it such.

Introduction

Starting a business is like mining for gold. Each business is like discovering a new mine in search of gold. To keep your business going you continually chip away, some days finding new gold i.e. making money. On other days finding nothing i.e. making no money, however as an entrepreneur you keep chipping away, and when that gold mine is no longer producing, you move on to mine somewhere else.

I decided to write this book because many people approach me daily and ask lots of questions about being in business, employing people, marketing, sales, research, and other related questions that they do not have answers to from elsewhere.

So, I thought I could put together a book that can recount my experiences over many years of being in business. This book would be available for people to purchase, and then read and work through the different queries they have, at their own pace.

There are many books on self-employment so why should this book be any different? Why should you be interested in my experiences? I think the difference with this book is that I include my moral compass which in my case is guided by a social conscience and using my spare time to become involved in community work and charities.

When starting this book, it was all about how to become self-employed, like a business guide. A colleague of mine who has written her own books, said to me "why don't you put some things in the book that are about you, people find it interesting reading about people and people's lives", and so that is what I did.

One of the realisations I came to when writing this book, is how many things from my past I have been able to recall, which is all a part of my experience. The book is a realistic recount of real events, and examples of experiences I have been through.

It might encourage you to know why I pursued business despite having a difficult start. You see, school never taught me about life. I struggled with knowing where and how I fitted in, and the more I struggled, the more I realised that experiencing real life is a lot different to being told about it. We are not all the same so why are we all taught in the same way at school?

After leaving school, I felt like a square plug trying to fit into a round hole, going nowhere fast. In a way I didn't find self-employment, self-employment found me, as I was wondering the wilderness between adolescence and adulthood. At the time, I was thinking I should have done better at school, I should have listened to my parents, I should have been more focused, I should have stayed on at sixth form, gone to college and university.

Eventually, I attended university as a part-time mature student.

I feel blessed that I took the step into self-employment at this crossroads in my life. It has truly fitted my work ethic, personality, and character. As a non-conformist, the 9 - 5 office job did not suit me.

Looking back at my experiences now, I think some have been quite funny, some of them scary, and some very interesting, but the one thing I have learnt throughout this journey, is how the people we meet can have a real impact upon us. I have met people who have helped to change my negative feelings regarding people, places, or other things, to more positive feelings, and I hope this can be the same for you.

Sometimes, we get so consumed with the news that we think all is doom and gloom. Whether you are a million-aire, a micro businessperson, or someone who lives on the streets, there are many more things in life than what you are currently exposed to. As a human, you will expe-rience love, fear, laughter, tears, and many other emo-tions. These are all important life experiences.

Being a businessperson is just another choice of career. You take the good with the bad, and you keep chipping away. The rewards are not always monetary, sometimes the reward is not anything we expect it to be, but all the same there are rewards, and on the balance of things I would say that there is more good than there is bad in business, more positive than negative.

Writing this book has undoubtedly been a challenge and a gift to me. Yes, it has taken up more than two years of my already busy schedule, however it has given me the opportunity to look back on where I started, and the twists and turns of the journey so far. I include the good, the bad, and the ugly here, and I hope it helps you to move forward on your business journey.

LEADERSHIP QUALITIES

HONESTY

DETERMINATION

INTEGRITY

COMPASSION

HUMILITY

CONFIDENCE

Chapter 1
Leadership

Many of us have all the traits of an entrepreneur, however we have not identified them, or worked on understanding them. Not only do we need to tease out our practical skills, we also need to tease out our hidden talents, that can be used to make our self-employment experience a successful one.

You are the person behind your business, its success depends on you! Write down all the things that you have been successful in, and use these successes to boost your confidence, because success is success, however you look at it.

What is success, moreover how do we define success? Is it owning a nice home, a nice car, expensive clothes, paying your bills on time every month, having savings, and going on holiday twice a year? Success can mean different things to many people, but the real issue here is no one seems to argue about identifying those who are successful, there seems to be universal agreement worldwide of who is successful.

Since it does not seem to be an exact science, how can it be so difficult to become successful? Your success can be in stages or milestones. Why not draw yourself a set of milestones and tick them off as you reach each one. You set them, you will know the distance between them and how realistic they are. Real life has a way of throwing obstacles in our way every time we are doing well; reset your milestones every now and then if you need to, but do not give up.

Later in the book, I will share some practical examples of starting from nothing, with little or no money, and making a success of yourself. We are not talking million-pound businesses here, although it is up to you how far you take things. We are talking about earning the average income if you were working full time and having the freedom to do it in your way, on your terms.

Once you become self-employed, you will begin to develop your ability to accept uncertainty. This is a definite part of being self-employed. Your creativity will see you through. Keep yourself motivated by your long-term ambition. Dig deep because with your perseverance, nothing will get in your way.

Every time you get knocked down, get up, brush yourself off, and go again. It is not the knock down that counts, it is what we do when we get up that matters.

Leadership is the one unique talent that I believe anyone needs to run their own business. Sometimes we get the meaning of leadership and management mixed up.

Managers manage by getting directions from leaders, and leaders lead. Being self-employed, having your own business and being a leader, requires similar skills to someone leading an organisation, a group of people, a band, a team, a community group, or a country.

One of the things a leader does, is to set the direction in which they are going, guide any staff, and employ managers to manage the staff. The person with the leadership skills would also have the authority to make decisions about the business. For example, one person will operate the business, set the parameters and the strategic direction within which the business will run (the leader), whilst the other person would employ people (the manager).

As a leader, you still have authority over what you are doing, and can direct the business where you wish for it to go, but you must ensure that if you take on any managers, they can continue in the same direction.

I think leaders need the skills to be able to take on advice, as sometimes things can go wrong because they think they know everything. I can assure you, taking advice and making sure you have the right team around you is especially important. When one leader consults with another this brings about a different perspective. It is important to act on the good advice you get, take time, and have an open mind.

As much as you can, you need to maintain control of what you do. Some of the things you do might involve having a licence, and with these licence's you need to make sure you are working within the law, and ignorance is no defence. Be sure you know the rules and regulations around any business that you start, and if you are an employer, please get someone on board who knows about employment legislation.

Even though you may take on professional advisers, i.e. lawyers, accountants, and such, you as the leader are still responsible for what you do. You must make sure that you know what you are doing because everything starts with you. Gain respect from, and respect those that you work with.

To be a leader, to be the person with the most power, you must realise that it comes with great responsibility. Be responsible about what you do, and lead yourself and your team, to greater things.

One of my first self-employed roles was working as a doorman; this required both leadership and patience. I worked in night clubs, bars, and hotels. I would go to work dressed in my black suit and tie and stand at the door deciding who comes in and who goes out. If there were any fights at the venue, I would be the first to go and break them up.

I would start work promptly at 9.00 pm, when working on the door, and finish at around 3.00 am. Most of the issues would be dealing with drunk people, so as a doorman I would have to find some way of getting them out of the venue, and into the street without them falling or hurting themselves or others.

Sometimes, we would have to break up fights between men or women, who were under the influence of alcohol. Sometimes we would even be breaking up fights between boyfriend and girlfriend. In a way, we were like unofficial police officers in charge of keeping people safe. I defended myself after being attacked on a few occasions, and without anyone getting hurt.

The job came with a bit of kudos on the streets. When I met people that I had not seen for years, and told them what I did, they kind of looked up to me. It was also good to meet up with other guys doing door work as it felt like our own community. There were few women doing door work back then. There are many more now.

One of the benefits of the job was that customers would buy us drinks. As I do not drink alcohol, they would get me soft drinks. Some of the other guys would get alcoholic beverages bought for them, after their shift had ended.

I remember on bank holidays, and public holidays, getting double time in terms of pay. This helped me to focus and realise I can work when others are having fun, which is useful for self-employment.

Now, let me take you back to the beginning, right back to the very start...

Chapter 2
Problem Child

Some time ago during the 1960's, a young woman went into labour at her home. An ambulance was summoned, and she was taken into the ambulance in Greenwich, London, to the hospital.

Whilst she was in the ambulance, the baby inside her decided that he was not going to wait until he got to the hospital, and so there in the ambulance, he was born.

That was the first time that my mother knew that she had been carrying a *problem child*, me! Imagine that, she then got to the hospital and the medics put her into the elevator with me, and the elevator got stuck. Somehow, the engineers and hospital staff were able to rescue me from the elevator. They took me onto the baby ward, yet the young woman, my mother who had just given birth, was left stranded in the elevator for some time. What a beginning to this unique journey.

Weighed, and subsequently described as a bouncing 8lb 1oz baby boy, who my mother and father named Keith!

I was a healthy baby, so my mother and I were allowed home shortly after. I was my mother and fathers third child. There was also my sister Monica who was one year, and my sister Paulette who was three years old.

Over the next few years, my mother had four more children, her last being a boy, so I was now one of seven children, two boys and five girls. I am the eldest son. That is the beginning of my story.

We moved to Reading whilst I was a baby, and we lived in two rooms in a shared house, with my dad's sister and her husband. Because both my mother and father were working, they were soon able to get a mortgage and buy a house.

Imagine seven children under ten! We used to sleep sideways across a double bed, all in one room as my parents shared the other room. My parents had rented two rooms in a house.

My father worked as a painter and decorator, and my mother a nurse, when I was young. So, the examples have been there, they were already set, regarding a good work ethic.

As I was a nightmare, I do not know how my parents coped. At one point I decided, whilst my parents were not in the room, to remove the fire guard; we had coal fires back in the day, with fire guards to guard the fires, and I tried to toast some bread on the fire in the room, holding the bread with a kitchen fork. I was not very good at this and somehow whilst I was toasting the bread, it caught fire, then my pyjamas caught fire, and eventually after the screams my parents came to my aid.

It was bad enough for me to have to spend some time in hospital.

That was not enough excitement for me, so I proceeded some months later, to swallow a number of pills when my parents were not looking. I had to be rushed to the hospital to get my stomach pumped out, so I was told. I was a handful, but I was not intentionally trying to be this problem child; I was forever trying things out.

When I got a little older, my father had a minibus, and I remember that we were parked outside my cousin's house. All seven children were in the minibus, whilst my father went to knock the door to see if my cousin was in. I climbed into the front and decided to let the handbrake down. I got out, went to the front of the minibus, and tried pushing it. My father came back, and he was furious. I do not know what it was that made me so curious about doing things and trying things out, but it was part of my personality, a part of my character.

I attended Groveland's Primary School, and by then we had moved to a new house again. Throughout my primary school life, I felt that I did not quite fit in. However, it is when I started The Meadway Secondary School at age eleven, that I started to find my feet. It was in secondary school when I started knowing that I wanted to be different.

As siblings, we always had our friends coming around to meet up before we went to school or coming around to play after school. We always had food, drink, clothes, games, and toys. It is when I became an adult, that I understood more about the challenges that my parents went through.

My brother, sisters, and I, were really close growing up. I have some of the most amazing memories of our childhood, the laughter, the messing about, the getting told off, all those things you do when there are seven children, and that is what I believe kept us close.

When I started secondary school, my maternal grandparents lived with us, and then afterwards, my paternal grandparents. We have a big family, and we would always have extended family over too. We really enjoyed those fun times.

At the time, we used to walk to school, over a mile from where we lived in Groveland's Road. Groups of us would meet in the morning, and part of our enjoyment would be that journey to school. We would walk to the bottom of the road to a housing estate, through the housing estate into a woodland, through the woodland, and we would come out not too far from our school. This was a daily occurrence, and on our way back from school it would probably take us three times as long, because we did not have any time constraints and we would play hide and seek in the woods and so on. I have fond memories of all of this.

Chapter 3
Your Mindset

During my secondary school years, my mother and father both worked at Mars. My father started working there first. The great thing about it was that every week when my father got paid, he would bring back bags of sweets; quite a lot of Mars sweets such as: Bounty, Mars, Milky Way, Topic, and Twix. I would have a bag once a week; I would go to school and sell the sweets individually in the playground.

Being one of seven children, I received little pocket money and therefore I had a paper round. So, the fancy trainers, going out on trips and visiting London, would be funded by my own money from doing the paper round.

At the time, I did not realise that this was my first business experience, in terms of becoming self-employed. The main reason I did it was not just to make money, but also to make friends. The guy with the chocolate bars in the playground was a popular guy. I did not put much thought into it, and have not thought much about it since, but I can see how important it was to my life. I think that this decision was the very start of me becoming a businessperson.

Back in those days I used to collect matchbox cars, which were little metal replicas of real cars. A friend of mine reminded me some time ago, that I promised myself when I got older, I would buy the real cars. I was not thinking back then, that by the time I got older, those cars would be too old and might not be the current models anymore, but those were the types of things I would buy with my money.

I did not need to do any marketing because people at school were always in the playground at breaktime, so I had a captive audience, I also got a lot of repeat business.

At school, I played in the Meadway School Steel Band. We would usually play out on a Saturday, and we once played on a television programme called 'Hey look that's me'.

Leaving school and entering the big wide world of work is one hell of a step. Some young people take the challenge on the chin and embrace the adult way of doing things. Others find it too daunting and spend months, sometimes even years, being unemployed, this is where a positive mindset can step in saying to you, 'you go for it, because you can do it'. 'Whatever your mind can conceive, you can achieve if you believe'.

This should enable you to pull yourself out of the depths of self-doubt and move you towards self-empowerment.

When you encounter challenges and you go to an expert to help you solve your issues, these experts do not necessarily have all the answers, sometimes it is just about you and who you have been around, and what information and materials you have been exposed to. This information is what can make you realise that you already had the answer.

What if I could show you a way? Or could prove to you, that you already possess all the skills that you need? And also make you believe that it is not so difficult, what if I could show you that it does not cost much money to start off on your own, that you do not have to borrow? In fact, you need extraordinarily little money to start off on your own and become successful. It is just about patience and perseverance. What if I could show you that you could start changing your life from next month? Or even next week? Could you? Would you? What would it take to convince you?

Until you believe you can do this, you will not really move from your current mindset. Remember this is not a get rich quick scheme, it is about experienced people like me, showing you examples of how we became entrepreneurs from very humble beginnings. You can start off slowly and in time become highly successful in business.

As you may be aware, there is a difference between someone that says they can do it, and someone that believes they can do it. It is not about words; it is about actions. Throughout this book you will read about different examples of my very own business experiences. For instance, I have been to a business conference where the host said to the audience 'what if I showed you a proven business concept that you can try out, but before you try it, go and show the business concept to an accountant or solicitor, to verify if it is financially viable and legal'. I went to the conference in a positive frame of mind and left even more positive. I tried it, and it worked.

Sometimes, when people are in a chronic state of helplessness regarding work, or earning, they turn to the criminal element, thinking that by getting involved in crime that this can somehow help catapult them into a financially secure position. This is a myth.

What we are talking about is not looking over your shoulder, worrying, causing yourself any extra stress, or ripping anyone off, but just knuckling down, following a few basic steps, looking at who you have around you, what friends and family surround you, and who your friends and family have around them. By tapping into your own networks, that perhaps you did not know you had, you can get to a position where you start earning decent money for yourself and your family.

I have read and spoken to people that have embarked upon get rich quick schemes. Those books sell by the bucket loads because they make people believe that they work. Sometimes when you are down, you want to hold onto anything that you believe can turn your life around and bring you out of your financial situation, and into a situation where you are no longer worrying.

Changing your mindset from negative to positive is something that you should try to do. Reading books about positive people and topics could really get you on your way. What have you got to lose?

Chapter 4
And the Winner is...

Fifteen years old, full of energy, full of attitude, a pain in the butt for most of my teachers, not taking school, or my pending exams seriously enough, looking forward to leaving school and not having a clue of what would be in store for me.

I spent most of my time when I was not in school, riding my racing bike. I would race it with friends and when we were not racing each other, or running up and down, we would have sprint challenges by the housing estate near where I lived.

I had one thing going for me – speed. I could sprint, but I never took it seriously enough, like with everything I was involved with then. During my last year at secondary school we had a sports day, and each person could compete in a maximum of three disciplines in athletics, either two fields and one-track event, or two track and one field event. I chose the one hundred metre sprint, the two hundred metre sprint, and the triple jump.

As this was my last sports day, I put some effort in. I came first in the one hundred metres, first in the two hundred metres, and second in the triple jump. The guy I came second to in the triple jump, came second in two of his disciplines, so when all the points were totted up at the end of the sports day, I was the person in my school year with the highest number of points. I was presented with a trophy, which in today's equivalent is 'Sports Personality of the Year'. The trophy was for the person who scored the most points.

And if that was not enough, I learnt that my one hundred metre sprint was timed at eleven, point one second, and that I had broken my school's longstanding sprinting record. It was announced on three occasions on the last sports day at my school, *"And the winner is... Keith Seville"*.

Each year Reading secondary schools would meet at Palmer Park Stadium, with its state of the art running track, and covered seating area for spectators.

I was on form, fresh from my school record breaking sprint. I was chosen to run the one hundred metres representing my school, and the 4 x 100 metres relay. This was the biggest stage I had competed on, and now with my new record-breaking running spikes (trainers). As far as I can remember, I came third in the one hundred metres sprint final. The final track event of the day was the 4 x 100 metres relay and I was the last person in my team to run taking the baton to the finish line. We lined up in our lanes waiting nervously.

Bang! The starter pistol went off, we had a brilliant start. Then the baton was handed to the second runner in our team who ran around the bend. We were in a great position, neck, and neck with the other team at the front, then the second handover and my running mate was coming around the corner. It looked like we were just in the lead, all I had to do was start running within the designated zone, take the baton and run like my life depended on it. With my hand stretched out behind me, I squeezed my fist to feel for the baton, accelerated and the baton fell! I was accelerating without it, we were disqualified, and I was gutted.

Looking back now, at the speed I had ran then at such a young age, I am sure if I had taken sprinting seriously, I could have perhaps represented England in athletics. I am confident that with the correct training, I would have been able to reduce my time by up to 1.5 seconds and become a competitor for a world championship medal.

However, I did not do that, I did not take it seriously and I do look back thinking 'what if?' These could be quite important signs as to the type of person I was, even though at the time I did not realise it. Some things came naturally to me, and if I put my mind to it, I would be quite good. If there is something you feel you could achieve without putting too much work in, imagine what you could achieve if you really did put the work in. Just imagine...

I sometimes ask myself, could there be a link between me winning on the track and winning in business? As I said before, at fifteen years old, I had no idea what I wanted to do as a career once I left school.

I did not follow up on my breaking the one hundred metre record at school. One of the ways I could have developed this ability would have been to join an athletics club and take running more seriously. However, instead, I left school and left the one hundred metres record behind and never looked back. Come to think of it, I was hopeless at long distance running, I did not even try to be good at it. In my opinion, it took too long from start to finish. Maybe it was a case of impatience or it could have been stamina, I never did find the underlying cause.

I remember some years later, when Linford Christie won the world sprint one hundred metres championship gold, and the Olympic one hundred metre gold for Great Britain. I wondered what speed he was running the one hundred metres back when he was fifteen years old. Knowing that information, would mean that I could have been a contender.

School is a place where you study and hope to leave with enough qualifications to go to sixth form or college, and eventually university, before you embark on a career path to take you into your mature years. It does not fully prepare you for life in the real world.

I spent most of my secondary school years living in a place called Tilehurst in Reading, Berkshire. During the last year of my schooling I moved with my family to a place called Cemetery Junction, in the same town.

I became close with three guys, Timmy, Alfred and Andrew, and we referred to ourselves as 'the lads'. I knew Timmy previously, because my family knew his family, and our paths crossed a few times, before he introduced me to his friends Alfred and Andrew.

We as four young men were extremely competitive, we would compete against each other all the time. We enjoyed running, sprinting, long distant races, and play fighting. However, if you were watching, you might think we were really fighting. We went to the gym, and we would each try to lift the most weights, and we would also arm wrestle against each other. We would also try out gymnastics without any formal teaching, trying back and front flips, pushing each other's shoulders down with our legs spread to see if we could do the splits and see who could go down the further to the ground. On top of that we would enter disco dancing competitions.

We really enjoyed each other's company and we saw each other as often as we could. When we left school, we all decided to meet in Friar Street, a place in Reading, and we talked about how successful we would be in the future. Thirty-five years later, we do not see each other as often as we used to growing up, however responsibilities become our focus. What I can say for sure is that for at least the last twenty years, all of us have run our own businesses and have been employing staff, and all of us are still self-employed.

Coming from a working-class background and going to a regular secondary school, we didn't know the direction of life, or business, at the point when we left school.

We knew about being competitive and staying competitive, and I believe that is what has driven all of us. When I meet up with the lads, individually, or a couple of us, we can really laugh, deeply belly laugh about the things we got up to when we were growing up. We were in and out of each other's houses as if we were one family living at four different addresses. Our parents saw our friends as much as their own children every day, we were so close like four brothers. So, I think if you have vision, commitment and are competitive, those three ingredients put into the mixing pot can help you become an entrepreneur.

It was conforming in the outside world that I had a problem with, and the rules of working for a company, and the maturity that it required of me.

Whether in, or out of school, I had a problem conforming to the rules. This challenge was the same when working for a company. Since I could not work for anyone else, it seemed the best solution was to work for myself.

Chapter 5
Frogs and Trogs

Frogs and Trogs, what on earth could this chapter be referring to, you may be thinking?

Well I can put you out of your misery, *Frogs and Trogs* is the name of a disco business that I was involved with in the early 1990's, and I will tell you how the name came about. There were three of us, all friends in secondary school, involved in this disco business, Michael, James, and me, and we were known as Slick (myself), Mick (Michael) and Sugar Browne (James).

Those were our nicknames in school however the name Frogs and Trogs came about because some people used the nickname 'froggy' when referring to Michael. I am sure he would not mind me saying, but some people called him 'froggy' because he had quite big eyes.

So, Frogs and Trogs should have in fact been called Frog and Trogs, because Michael was the frog, and myself and James were the trogs (followers).

We would hire some of the latest twin deck turntables, we would hire amplifiers, speakers, a microphone, sometimes echo chambers, smoke machines, the whole lot, and we would get bookings and go and play at different disco's or create our own and get paid for doing so.

At the time, we had a rival disco tech called 'Take Six Boys' and they were made up of six guys that we grew up with. Some of them went to our school, but they were all guys we knew as we would sometimes see one another at discos we were attending.

Sometimes, we would play at the same events and challenge each other in terms of who had the best records, the latest records, and who had the most people dancing to their records.

Although I didn't see it at the time, this was another example of a business, going out, getting hired and being paid to provide a service.

In Frogs and Trogs we did it almost like a hobby, we loved music, so we would go out and play. We did not really have a business plan, we did not really have a plan, we did not even realise it was a business. Sometimes, we would get a bit of hassle about getting paid, then we would hassle people about us not getting paid, or not getting paid enough.

Putting on a disco now, is quite different to how it was back then. We had large boxes of old records, big speakers, and all sorts of equipment. Nowadays, the equipment is a lot smaller and has built in speakers. Despite their size they are much more powerful.

Looking back, there have been a few examples of me being involved in a business or employing myself, or a group of us setting up a business, and we just did not see it as that.

But it was all fun. We had a laugh and it was a fantastic time. I am still in touch with Michael and James, not as often as we were when we were younger, but we are still in contact.

Prior to Frogs and Trogs, I was employed to do a paper round. I did not realise how significant it would be in terms of grounding me for a lifetime in self-employment.

As I start thinking about those times, all the memories have come back. I remember I would come home from school, take off my school uniform, rush down to the paper shop, which was a mile away, and collect my pile of newspapers. I would know which one was for my road as it would have the road name and numbers on it, so I would stack them in my bag and then go on my way.

The basic routine would be to open entrance gates, walk up paths, put the paper through the letter box, and repeat this at the other houses along the road. The good thing was that the roads were quite close together, so I would go up one road, down one side, then the other side, before going to the next road and so on.

Although it only took a few hours, it felt like it took forever, and I sometimes felt that I was walking extremely far, even though it was not very far in distance. It was worse when it was raining, snowing or icy. No one likes slipping in the snow, and sometimes it got bad. On a sunny day it always worked out better.

Thinking back, I recall that the bags were quite heavy. I could be opening the gate and there would be a barking dog coming towards me, I would be running with this heavy bag out of the gate, and normally the dog's owner would call for the dog and they would get the paper from me or come out when they heard their dog barking. I never got bitten by any of the dogs I used to see, but I did have a few close calls.

The winter evenings were very cold, and it would get dark quickly. At times, I must admit it was quite scary. When the shift was done, I would take the bag back to the paper shop and be so glad when it was time to go home, to be in the warm.

I would do the paper round five days a week, and at the end of the second week, I would get paid. The shop keeper would try and work out how many papers I had delivered to people's houses and I was always short changed. The shop keeper would tell me there were clients who said they had not received their paper, so I would not get money for those as the cost of those papers would be deducted from my wages.

It was years later that I realised that it was a way the shop keepers could keep money, rather than give it to us kids that were doing the paper rounds. I never really complained about it, it was nice having my own money to top up my pocket money, and again it was an experience that at the time I did not really investigate, but I know it served me well, as it taught me about having a good work ethic.

Alongside the paper round, I worked in a hotel. My first experience in a hotel was as a young 14-year-old, helping my mum to wash up. She had a part time job, and would take myself, and one or two of my sisters along to help her.

I had never ever been into such a large kitchen, and I had never seen so many big pots and pans. We would soak, and scrub them, for what seemed a very long time. It used to take us all evening to get everything clean and then the chefs that worked in the hotel's restaurants would make us some nice grilled food to end the evening.

So, I had a disco business, paper round weekday evenings, and washing up at a hotel some evenings after my paper round, and then waking up early to go to school the next morning. As a young person I was busy, and hardworking in the world of work.

Chapter 6
Urban Warrior

I learnt to play classical guitar at school, and when I left school, I took to playing the guitar more seriously. I decided to buy a bass guitar. At the time my mum got it for me out of a catalogue, which I was responsible for paying off every week. I had no idea what kind of opportunities this guitar would give me.

One day I had a call from a friend of mine, who said that there was a new band getting together, and that the bass guitarist did not turn up. I went to rehearsals a couple of times and started playing my guitar, and as they say, the rest is history.

We formed a band called *Urban Warrior* and performed at local venues in the beginning, eventually going for an audition in London, to be involved in an international tour. We did not get through the audition process the first time.

A year later, we had a second chance to audition for the same company, there were loads of bands involved. This time we won!

Playing in an audition along with some top bands in London, and being a band from little Reading, sometimes known as 'country' by the Londoners, was a real achievement, especially when we won. Within a few weeks we had packed our bags and were off to Sudan, in Africa. There were eight of us in the band. We were in Sudan for one month, staying in a hotel and playing at different venues around the country.

I had never been to Africa before, and I think only one of our colleagues that we were travelling with had done so. We landed in Khartoum, the capital of Sudan. It was night-time, it was pitch black. The aeroplane door opened, and we were in single file walking down the aisle. I had my jacket on because it was so cold on the aeroplane, but when I got to the door, I could not believe the heat, it was almost unbearable.

Before this experience, I had only related heat to daytime sunlight, but this was night-time and in darkness. It was like a major fan heater waiting for us at the airport. We were soon taken to an air-conditioned hotel where we stayed whilst in Sudan.

I had not expected Africa to be built-up. Geography was not my strongest subject at school. I remembered teachers at school referring to African villages as being full of mud huts, so it was great for us to be staying in a five-star hotel, in built up modern Khartoum.

We would walk to go shopping or be taken by car to the venues where we would be performing, and we would be confronted by many children who were begging.

That saddened us quite a lot. We played at some major venues where there were many hundreds and thousands of people and it was extremely rewarding. At the time, we were told we were the first reggae band to visit Khartoum from the UK. After a month it was time to return to England, but it was an exceptionally good experience.

One of our singers was a manager of a local community centre, and we used to have band practice there between two to four nights a week.

In Urban Warrior we became good friends. We all had different personalities, and different characters, but our love for music was the glue that brought us together.

After work, we would practice throughout the night, as we really took it seriously. We also performed in France, and Germany.

An opportunity came for us to tour Tokyo, the capital of Japan. We jumped at the chance and stayed in Japan for four weeks. We were provided with an apartment and were able to come and go as we pleased.

Japan had a different culture to what any of us had ever experienced before. The atmosphere, weather and people were all quite different. Everyone was friendly, and it was a wonderful experience. I have never eaten seafood as often as I did during the month we were in Japan. We would ask the tour manager to get us familiar foods, like Cornflakes, Weetabix, KFC, and things that we were used to.

We performed most nights and it really was a different experience on stage. From a group of friends playing music, to a group of guys living in an apartment; it was not all plain sailing. Sometimes we would have our little disagreements, but overall, it was a good atmosphere.

The main difference between being in the heart of Japan, and the heart of London, was how orderly everyone seemed to be. For example, everyone would gather at the side of the road, and cross the road together unlike in London, where people would cross the road whenever they wanted to. In Japan, it seemed that people tend to use taxi cabs more than in England; their yellow cabs were a lot more popular than our black cabs.

The audience really showed their appreciation and so did our tour manager. We were really treated as celebrities while we were in Japan; the experience was good.

Being in a band in my opinion, is just like being in business; we would participate, perform, use our expenses to hire a van, PA system, microphones, and fuel for the van. When we got paid, we would split the money with the other band members and the manager.

In business, you may get someone that works in the office doing administration, someone who does finance, and someone who does sales. In a band, someone sings, someone plays guitar, someone plays the drums, and someone plays keyboard.

Although it was a small part of my life growing up, I realise how much work my friends and I put into it. We played big venues like the main stage at Notting Hill

Carnival, Stonehenge Festival, and we also performed at Reading Hexagon alongside major acts like Curtis Mayfield.

We also did some recording at Streatley on Thames and met with the manager of The Human League. We made some waves, and our name was being recognised in the music world. As we were not earning much money, we all decided that we would go and get so-called 'proper' jobs.

Those of us that were in the band sometimes bump into each other, and when we do, we often reminisce about the band.

When Urban Warrior ceased as a band, myself, Welch, a friend from Urban Warrior, and Michael, my friend from Frogs and Trogs, formed another band called 'Freestyle'.

Freestyle was different in that we performed without musical instruments, we wrote and recorded songs, and backing tracks at a recording studio, and all three of us would perform and sing. Michael was the lead singer, Welch and I would harmonise, and our backing tracks would play in the background.

Freestyle did not have to carry large pieces of equipment like Urban Warrior, just microphones. We continued with Freestyle for a few years, had some of our own records pressed, and then we came to a point in life where we decided that it was time to hang up the microphones.

Like they say, 'all good things must come to an end', and this chapter ended, so another one could begin.

If we believe

I know we can do it
How long we've been searching to do it right
Whatever our minds can conceive

We can achieve
If we believe
If we believe

Somehow someday we'll find a way
Don't let nothing stop you
Or stand in your way
You've got to hold your head up high
And reach the sky

We can achieve
If we believe
If we believe

Song lyrics written by M Romeo, W Henderson, K Seville
'Freestyle Band' - circa 1988

Chapter 7
Job to Job

On leaving school, it was inconceivable that I could be unemployed, as my parents were totally opposed to it. If I thought that on leaving school, I would get a break and have a lie-in, I was in for a rude awakening. Every day, my mother and father would make sure I got up early, had a bath, got dressed and was out looking for work.

The first job I had was working for a major bathroom showroom. People would tend not to come into the showroom, so we would end up walking around looking for customers who were seldom there. Because the job was so boring at times, during breaks I would sometimes nod off.

I had just left school aged 16, and I remember being called into the office by one of the managers, who gave me a telling off for falling asleep in the staff room during my breaktime. I thought that was quite bizarre as I was on my break and not in view of any customers. The other problem was we were required to work on Saturdays, and at the time I was still in my school steel band, and we used to perform on Saturdays. We would travel to play at different places and events.

Management were unhappy that I had to take the day off on a Saturday to play for the steel band. Eventually I had to quit my job because it was clashing with my steel band playing.

I got my second job after leaving school, which was working for a major supermarket. I remember wearing a long blue mac as a part of my uniform and going around sticking prices on different foods. I remember feeling really embarrassed when I would bump into people that I knew from school, sometimes I would hide down the aisle for them not to see me.

The main reason that job did not last, was because I could not see myself in that role, and once you cannot see yourself doing something, you really start feeling like you should not be there. It took its toll, and I then decided it was not for me.

I felt after leaving school, that even though I was not the best qualified in terms of the CSE/GCE qualifications, that I would not end up working in a shop, pricing up goods, and stacking shelves.

I got a new job at an electro plating factory that were metal finishers. They chrome plated metal, using a lot of acid and other substances. We would have to wear a lot of protective clothing such as overalls, gloves, and goggles. I worked there for a while, but I could not see a future for me there, so I got another job as a trainee welder.

As a trainee welder, I knew I would be able to obtain a qualification. However, as it was my first year after I left school, I was still young, and I was still going to discos.

One evening, I was at a disco speaking to a young lady and she asked me if I had been by a fire or if I have been burning anything, and I said, 'no I haven't' and she said, 'it smells like you have', and that made me very conscious about the smell.

After we finished welding, we used a gel called Swarfega to wash our hands. It seemed that no matter how many times I washed my hands with the Swarfega, and showered and used my sprays to smell nice, I would still always smell like I was burning, so I had to knock that job on the head.

My fifth job was working for an office equipment company, and that was an apprenticeship. It was an interesting job because we would go around servicing and repairing electric typewriters. They were mainly golf ball and daisy wheel typewriters, and we would go and repair the machines as part of a service contract for the company that I worked for.

At the start of the second year of my apprenticeship I attended Merton Technical College in London, one day a week. I started to learn about electronics. At the company I worked for whilst doing my apprenticeship, we moved on from repairing typewriters to calculators and dictating machines, which I found really interesting. The business closed shortly after I completed my apprenticeship and I found myself job hunting again.

In the third year after leaving school, I went to a youth club, and they happened to be advertising a job for a

Court Welfare Officer. I read the person specification, job description and thought, 'yeah, I could get into this'.

I was glad that I got the job. It was about helping young people that were in the criminal justice system. Many of them were being put into prison and being detained without getting proper representation when they were going to court. My job was to go to the courts every morning and talk to some of the young people that had no solicitors by their side and ask them a few questions to find out if they would like to be represented and explain to them the benefits of representation.

I was based at a community centre, and the job was funded by Urban Aid, a major government fund at the time, so I was employed by the local authority, the then Berkshire County Council. I would get names, addresses and phone numbers from these young men and women and I would contact a solicitor's firm in London that we used. The firm specialised in criminal law. I would make appointments and then accompany the young people to the solicitors in London. They would explain their circumstances and provide the solicitor with court hearing dates and all the paperwork they had, and the solicitor would represent them in court.

I met a lot of young people through this work, and I was very surprised by the amount of young people that were willing to go to court and plead guilty to things that maybe they had not done, just to get out of the court. They used to have what they called TIC's where offenders would be given a list of offences that the police had not yet solved. The young person was told that if they admitted to doing the crimes, this would be taken into consideration in their sentencing, but they would not normally be sentenced for it. The police would list for example ten burglaries in an area and the people would say they had done it.

For getting into trouble with the police, many of these young people would find themselves evicted from their accommodation.

This is what made me decide that I should try and find a way of housing some of the young people. So, I started up a property business, which you can read about later in the book.

Chapter 8
From Mars to Benefits

A couple of years after I left school, I was in-between jobs, and this was scorned on by my parents.

At the time my father was working at Mars, a sweet factory in Slough, and the shifts were 6.00 am to 2.00 pm, 2.00 pm to 10.00 pm, and 10.00 pm to 6.00 am. The shift pattern was to work nine days on and then have three days off.

While I was in-between jobs my father said, 'Keith, there are some temporary jobs at Mars going, you must apply for one of them, it's a temporary job for three months'. Back in the day, you could not tell your parents you do not want to apply for the job packing sweets in a sweet factory, back in those days, you did what you were told.

I applied for the job and went to an interview. I did not put much effort in, but I got the job, and I worked at Mars packing 'Twix'.

The Twix would come along the conveyer belt. I would catch four Twix with one hand, and four with the other, and then pack them into a box, repeat the same again, and then put a cardboard piece in the box to divide the sweets from each other. When the box was full, I would put the lid on and start a new box.

Day in, day out, that is what we did. The advantage was with every hour or so we got a 15-minute break, and whilst we were in Mars we could eat as many sweets as we wanted, but we could not take them out of the factory. The disadvantage was that I felt like I was being haunted by Twix, in my sleep. I saw Twix coming down the production line in my dreams, and even in my daydreams.

I lived in Reading, and the Mars factory was in Slough. Mars provided their staff with coaches to come to work, so at 5.00 am we would catch the coach, and it would get us into work at approximately 5.40 am so that we could start work promptly at 6.00 am. When we had finished our shift, the coach would drop us back.

I was never used to getting up at that time in the morning, so I found it very difficult. The afternoon shifts were not too bad because we would catch the coach around 1.00 pm, but we would not get back till 11.00 pm. I would fall asleep on the coach going home, and then have a mile or so walk back to our house. I would go to sleep and once I woke up the day would be finished; I really did not think that factory work was for me.

My dad was a machine minder, which is called a main-tenance man these days. He would make sure the machines were working and if anything went wrong, he would fix them so that they were up and running again.

One of the things he said to me, was that if I really get my head down and do well with this temporary role, then at some stage I may be able to be a machine minder, just like him. That is the type of dad I had, he would always look out for me, but sometimes young people have different aspirations than their parents because the generations are different.

I remember one day there was an artist performing in Reading, one of the international artists that I had always wanted to see. On that night I was working a night shift, so I could not go out to see the artist with all my friends and have an entertaining night. It was at that point I thought that as soon as this three-month trial finishes I will be gone, and I will be looking for a daytime job, so I could have my evenings and nights to myself and continue to enjoy my life. Once the three months was up, I finished.

There were vacancies for people that wanted to try for permanent, full time jobs, but it was not a consideration I took on board. I do not think that my parents were incredibly happy about my decision, but that was the right decision for me.

After making the decision to leave home, I was forced to go down the route of benefits, so that I could pay to have somewhere to live, and I could buy some food to eat. I privately rented a flat in Langley, which is on the outskirts of Slough in Berkshire. Every 2 weeks I had to go to the benefit office and sign on and say that I was looking for work. I had to prove this by having several interviews each week. Even if I was not suited to those jobs, I still had to do that to keep receiving the money.

I believe the weekly benefit that I was receiving was hardly enough for me to manage on. When you hear the term 'being down on your luck'; that time in my life gave me an insight into understanding what that the term truly means. The way the benefit staff looked and spoke to me made me feel that I was not worth anything; they make you feel worthless.

I remember the trips to the benefit office on the bus, and I would look around me and see people who were also looking, and I thought 'wow, look at the state of them'. I was wondering all the time whether people were looking at me like that. You get forced into this group, and you just feel so helpless as you wait to receive your benefit money. I was one of the fortunate ones because I had clothes from when I was working, so I dressed respectfully.

One of the things that is important to know is, if you continue down that road in that negative system, going to that place every two weeks you can easily get stuck in the benefit trap. In my opinion, there is nothing that inspires you, or makes you feel any better about yourself, so sometimes you feel like that is it, that is where your life will end. I just knew it was not for me.

I knew whatever I had to do, I had to turn my life around, so I started putting together ideas on a piece of paper and I started researching business ideas. I put figures together, getting as much information as I could about what I knew to put together a business.

Chapter 9
Unemployable

Let me explain what I mean by '*unemployable*', how long I have had this condition, and how I developed it.

You see I am unemployable and am happy to admit it. Not in a bad way, I just have a problem conforming to the everyday norms. I am in no way suggesting that you are unemployable and that this book is written for people who are also in that position.

I have been running businesses in one way or another for many years and it has been like a rollercoaster with its ups and downs and dips and turns. However, I would not have it any other way.

I had five jobs in two years: sales assistant, apprentice welder, apprentice service engineer, factory worker and trainee financial advisor. Somehow it did not matter how good I felt I was doing in the job, the managers thought differently. I was well mannered, dressed appropriately, a good timekeeper, clean and tidy and a good communicator, however, I always either fell out of love with the job, or it fell out of love with me.

After many years of studying myself, I concluded that I have a condition of being unemployable, and the cure for my condition is self-employment. Do not get me wrong, I went to many interviews and got job offers, the interviews were not the problem.

From the intensity of the tests, and the information that was requested at interviews, you would think I was going for a job at some secret intelligence agency. The isometric tests, the psychological, sociological, and intellectual tests had me feeling brain dead at the end of some of the interviews. In fact, I believe that one of the interviews for a financial company left me with a mini nervous breakdown, I kid you not!

I believe it may have been those high-pressure interviews, those interrogation techniques, the middle-aged men in suits sat around the table staring at me, as if I was at a police station interview, that gave me cause to try something new. Each question they asked me, I was tempted to say, 'no comment', or 'can I call my solicitor now please?' How dare they try to intimidate me like that! I suppose it all turned out well in the end otherwise I may have been trapped in some miserable dead-end job, with my pension, the only thing to look forward to.

What if the pension company goes bankrupt with hundreds of millions of pounds owing to pensioners, and there is no way of collecting the money to keep me through my retirement, whilst the former directors of the pension company are living in mansions and being driven by chauffeurs with yachts at their disposal.

This is a reality, and has happened, leaving many people of pensionable age with no pension, even though they had paid into a pension plan throughout their working life. Which is why I now manage my own business, whilst encouraging others to do the same.

Whatever the case, you must have an idea of your strengths and weaknesses to know how you would react to certain circumstances if you were self-employed.

I would suggest that you start by stripping away all the scientific gobbledegook you may read and get down to business. Take one step at a time whilst researching the process of getting started on your self-employment journey. Do not be put off by words such as entrepreneurial traits, as if there is some sophisticated thinking process to becoming self-employed. You have what it takes, so take what you have and get going!

Have you ever driven along the road in the early morning and looked at the faces of people going to work? You would think they are all on their way to Court to have a life sentence imposed! You do not have to be driving, you could be on the bus, train, bicycle or even walking; you will still see them the same, looking miserable and depressed.

Why would someone put themselves through that, day in, day out, week in, week out, year in, year out? Maybe, it is because of our schooling or upbringing.

However, one of the unique human gifts we have is that we can go against our scripting. We can reprogram our minds and start our own business, by first developing the mindset of the self-employed.

Sometimes, when you have been unemployed for long enough, you start to believe that you are unable to work and earn. The only problem with that negative approach, is that it could be a self-fulfilling prophecy. How many unemployed people do you think would like to be given a chance to prove to themselves, their families, and friends, that given the right opportunity, they will be able to turn their life around?

I truly believe that could be the case, and if this description fits you, I suggest that you take a punt because you can do it, but first you need to do some research. Whether it's searching online, or reading books, see if you can find out what the experts say about you changing your way of life, and getting out of the depths of unemployment, and getting out of that state of chronic helplessness. Pay attention to the positive people that can help you to see a way forward and avoid the ones that make you feel bad about your chances. Either way this can be a turning point. Check your skills, your knowledge, and the people you are exposed to because these things can have the biggest effect on you and your business.

However, until you believe you can do this, you will not really move from your state of unemployability. This is not a get rich quick scheme, it is about finding examples of how from very humble beginnings you can start off slowly but become remarkably successful in business. That is a reality.

There is a difference between someone who believes they can do it and someone who says they can do it; it is not about words it's about actions.

Chapter 10
Contact Sports

I was a member of 'Reading Amateur Boxing Club', I trained and fought in the light heavy weight division. I had a few fights until it was too much for me, and I had to choose between boxing and business.

One time there was a select team of us from England, that were chosen to box in the Isle of Wight, against a select team from the Isle of Wight. In my opinion, I won my fight. It was a pity that the referee saw it differently and gave the decision to my opponent, who was the home boy at the time. Despite this, it was a good experience.

Being an amateur boxer takes a lot of time, guts, training, and commitment, but unlike running my own business, boxing was more of a team sport. Yes, you would be in the ring by yourself, but anywhere Reading Amateur Boxing Club went and boxed, there would normally be a few of us that would be involved in a boxing match that night.

I boxed for a few years, then decided that it was not for me. The experience was brilliant, and I met some great people.

Even though I was involved in amateur boxing, I would discourage any son or daughter of mine to box. It sounds quite hypocritical I know; however, I think that any sport where you could hurt your opponent, especially by hitting them in places like the head or body to score points, is not a sport that I would want my children to participate in.

Boxing can seem like art when you watch people at the top of the sport, it can also get bloody and gory. I would rather be a spectator. That said I believe that boxing teaches you discipline, and in my opinion, it separates the men from the boys, in that you need to be strong mentally, and physically.

A couple of years after I quit boxing, I found myself with some spare time. I then started martial arts with the Apollo Karate Club, a well-established karate club that was affiliated to the Karate Union of Great Britain. The club is very well known, mainly for their fighting, and they enter many competitions throughout the year. It is a particularly good club to learn the basics of martial arts.

First, you buy yourself a white karate suit, and you start off with a white belt. Those who have been involved in martial arts, would know that you take different grades: a physical demonstration of the moves you learnt over the past few months. If you pass, you would be entitled to a different coloured belt that demonstrates your progress and level of ability. You train for three months, take an exam which if you pass qualifies you for your first coloured belt, if you do not pass you have to wait another three months to take the grading again. Each time you grade, you get a certificate and a stamp in your official grading book, with the date and time that you took your grading. The examiner would often be a respectable senior instructor from Japan.

It takes a minimum of three years to attain a black belt. There are also opportunities to continue your progress to a master level by further obtaining different degrees of black belt. You would train twice a week for at least an hour at a time.

There is a lot of stretching involved in training for martial arts and a lot of basic movements. Then when you are going to compete you would perform what they call free style or fighting.

I believe the boxing training put me in a good position when it came to practise martial arts because I was already quite fit. I fought through the ranks to junior instructor level.

A formidable team, we were seen as having some of the best individual fighters in the country in our group, and our instructors were well known in the martial arts community of Great Britain. I did it until I felt I could not dedicate myself to karate any longer.

Growing up, being the eldest boy, out of two boys and five girls in my family, I could do a lot of the girly things quite well, like skipping and rounders. I really felt in touch with my feminine side, growing up with five sisters, and when I went to secondary school and met other boys that had older brothers; I would think these boys were hard and tough. For me, boxing and martial arts was my way of experiencing my masculine side.

I used to play rugby when I was at school, so getting an opportunity to play for a local team in my early 30's, was very daunting, but exciting at the same time.

I decided to get myself a pair of rugby boots, and a rugby kit, and started to go to training. After the first few training sessions, I really felt like it was not going to work for me, but eventually I got through them, and we started to have regular games.

A lot of the players in the team had more experience than I did, they had played rugby for many years after they left school. They were a fantastic bunch of guys. We used to play at the Redingensians Rugby Club ground and went to Wales and all over the South of England to play the game.

This was my first experience of going out in sub-zero temperatures and playing rugby as an adult. Anyone who has played a winter sport knows that when the games kick off, the cold goes away, and you just get into the swing of things. We were running around, throwing the ball, and tackling people so we managed to keep warm.

Playing rugby and doing business sometimes does not always work well together. In one game I got tackled, someone fell on my leg and I tore a ligament. I got taken to the hospital on a stretcher and I had a plaster cast put on my leg from above my knee right down to my foot, which meant that I could not drive, and had to depend on people. For six weeks, my leg was in the plaster cast and it was exceedingly difficult for me to get on with anything.

After I had the plaster cast removed, it took some months before I was able to get back to normality, and that is when I realised that I was not so young anymore. Even when my leg had supposedly healed, whenever I would try to do some training, I would feel that ligament twitch with pain and discomfort. Eventually I had to give up playing rugby, and I took to training with weights to try and get back the strength in my leg. After doing that for some months, and then trying to play rugby again, I found that my ligament would still fail me. So that was the end of my rugby career.

I think it is very important to know that when you are older and get an injury, it is something that continues healing for a very long time, even when you forget about it, and it is never the same. It is as if that part of your body reminds you that it is different to when you were younger. It is something that hangs in there to always remind you not to extend yourself too much.

During the time of my leg injury, I had to depend on people, and I have never had to depend on people before. I had to ask them for lifts, and people would often be late, or unable to pick me up. I felt disabled, and vulnerable. In fact, I felt very down at the time, even though I tried not to show it.

Self-employment gave me the ability to construct my diary around my business and physio appointment times. It meant that I could manage my time more effectively than if I were employed.

Working all the hours you can, and at the same time trying to learn the ropes, does not just take mental fitness, it also takes physical fitness and I found that sport is a great way to learn this.

Chapter 11
Employing yourself

I just had an idea; it's about banning the business plan.

What do you reckon? It does what it says on the tin, ban the business plan. You can imagine, that someday, some guru came up with an idea to advise a would-be expectant mother or father to devise a baby plan.

Imagine the authorities advising women, that before they could have a baby, they must have a baby plan, and to bring the baby up into a respectable adult, the parents would have had to have followed the baby plan. How do you think that will go down in terms of human rights? There would be an uproar!

You get business advisors charging people all sorts of money, by saying 'I shall help you with your business plan'. It would be interesting to know if there is any research out there that can pinpoint accurately how many businesses start with a business plan, in comparison to those without a business plan. How many of those businesses succeed? And how many of them fail? As if the business plan is not enough, you get a business adviser telling you 'together with your business plan you need a marketing plan'. They may introduce you to one of their colleagues, who will then ask you to pay some more money, for them to put together a marketing plan.

I would also like to see some research, on how many business and marketing plans have succeeded, and how many have failed.

I am not implying that you do not need a plan. What I am saying is, you do not need an all singing and dancing business plan. I am not saying you do not need marketing; I am saying you do not need any kind of long-winded marketing plan. These plans are more for people who want to build multi-million-pound businesses.

Businesses with large turnovers that want to employ staff from the onset, and businesses that are looking to borrow money, should have a business plan that outlines each stage of their business and its growth. These plans will be used to show a potential bank or financial backer their processes and financial projections. Under these circumstances, they may also need a marketing plan.

Many people are forced to go into business, because they have not had the opportunity to work within a company and work their way up the ladder. This may include people in their 40's and 50's, who cannot get a job because they have been overlooked, in favour of those in their 20's.

Mothers with children are occasionally turned away from jobs. At their interviews they are given the impression that they are being fairly treated, but then the managers get together and say, 'no, we want an employee that will not take too much time off because of their children'. How many women of childbearing age are not getting jobs because managers are scared that they will have to take time off for maternity leave? These are the type of people that are not getting equal access to jobs and are not always treated well in the workplace.

People whose first language is not English, may not get as many job offers as a native person whose main language is English, because their command of English is not as good. When you look at all the different obstacles that are out there, you will realise that starting your own business on your own, and earning enough money to live off of, could very well be the way to go, and if you want to take it further then that is fine. However, business and marketing plans are not to be done to the extent that the adviser would be telling you to do it. There are simpler ways.

You should be able to put everything on a sheet of A4 paper, your business idea, and your overall direction. You do not need chapter and verse. Employing yourself means talking to yourself and taking yourself seriously, that may sound ridiculous, but it is true.

You become the employer and the employee. So, you can imagine how a disciplinary hearing would look, like *Keith Seville -vs- Keith Seville*; it would be something straight out of a comedy sketch. Hopefully it would never come to that; if it did, I would suggest you get some counselling, quick time.

The thing to remember is once you decide to work for yourself, you have already got over a major hurdle and the job is now yours.

Also, you do not have to worry about taking on employees or an office. You can choose to work from home and have a good level of control of when you work and when you have time off. There are some disadvantages, such as having no holiday or sick pay, and no one else to blame if you mess up.

Good health is essential when working for yourself. Get good rest and always be fresh and ready, even at short notice. It takes guts to become self-employed, and creativity to deal with the uncertainty this brings.

Identifying your strengths, weaknesses, opportunities, and threats as a self-employed person, can highlight something that you have overlooked. This could also help to identify what you need for commitment and focus. It takes time and energy, and it will do you the world of good going forward.

Managing yourself is an interesting concept because in my experience many of us believe that if we get into a situation, 'this is how I would deal with this', but when the situation arises, we deal with it differently.

The freedom of managing yourself may not be as easy as you first thought. A good analogy is travelling to a destination. You may go through many towns, each town gets you closer, and you finally arrive at your set destination. Sometimes, because of road works or the weather, you may be taken slightly off course, and you may get there a little later than you planned, or even a little earlier if the road is clear. The aim is to get to your destination, whatever the route and timeframe. So, you need the right attitude for your self-employment journey, there is no other way to say this; it takes hard work and perseverance.

Self-employment can be a lonely place and is the time you need to draw on your motivation. You need to be self-confident to accept uncertainty, and work to reach your goals. Throughout your journey you must be self-aware and identify areas for self-development. The way you conduct yourself must be conducive to the business environment.

For example, you should not be selling financial services wearing a baseball cap, your jeans hanging off your backside, wearing a football top from your favourite team. Or doing care work in a nursing home, in shorts and a bikini top. I am sure you are catching my drift. Dress appropriately for the work you are doing, taking into consideration health and safety, and the positive impression you want to leave with your clients. This stuff matters and helps you to be more successful.

Chapter 12
Kensington and Maidenhead

My father used to say to me, 'when things come easy, you do not appreciate them enough'. I used to think that it was just about when he would buy me new shoes or something else when I was young. I did not know that it would come back to haunt me in such a big way when I was an adult, when I was a grown man doing business.

However, it did, because I used to think that buying property was like playing a game of monopoly, and because I knew how to play it, how to get the deposit, the mortgage, the solicitors, and the surveyors, to put the whole thing together; that I was the man.

When I left school, I did not know much about business and mortgages. I do not know about you, but I did not even know, that I needed to know. I did not know about self-employment, about business strategies, and I had never heard of things such as mission statements, quality control, market research, and I did not even know there were such things as Business Coaches. The qualifications I attained in school were CSE's, I had a few of those, and I was then thrust into the outside world. However fast forward ten years, and I had started to dabble in the property market.

At the end of the 1990's I had been dabbling in properties for a few years, so I started travelling up to London on a week to week basis to make some more contacts. I met some estate agents, and property dealers, and eventually I found a property in a road just off High Street Kensington. I thought 'Yes, I have arrived!'.

I thought, property prices seem to be going up, properties seem quite expensive, so I will see if I can find a property that might need some work, get a mortgage, purchase it, and then do it up, turn it around and sell it, and make a profit. I could not get the mortgage on my own, so I drafted in my brother. So together, my brother and I, purchased this 3-bedroom, 2-bathroom, second floor apartment in Kensington Church Street.

As with many of my business ventures, I was juggling so many things at the time, that I was unable to concentrate on the flat. Also, my brother was working full time as a computer programmer.

We met and talked about what we should do with the flat. Eventually we decided we would not make a profit on the flat, and that we should just let it go, on the basis that we did not make a loss. All we lost on it in the end, was time, but what it did show me was that when you decide to purchase something to turn it around and make some money, that once you make the decision, the doing of it is not really that difficult.

The properties in that part of London have absolutely skyrocketed over the years and we would have made many tens of thousands of pounds profit from the venture. However, when you take on a venture, you also need to take on a team of people you can rely on, to see that venture through.

I was always searching for new business deals, and continually taking on things, even if I did not have the personnel within my grasp to see it through. Sometimes though, awfully expensive mistakes can lead to ideas that you can make vast amounts of profit from. I learned how to get involved in buying property in London, we viewed some really good properties, and learnt a little about the different areas in which to purchase properties and turn them around in a few months and make lots of money.

I also purchased a 6-bedroom property in Maidenhead, although the 6-bedroom property was incomplete at the time. It started as a 4-bedroom property. The owner was converting two rooms in the loft, and they basically ran out of money so were unable to complete it.

I raised a mortgage on the property and purchased it. I needed to do some work to finish off the two rooms. This time I was not going to turn it around to sell on; I wanted to run it as a bed and breakfast.

What happened next was, that the process of raising a mortgage and finding the deposit and so on and so forth, was quite a lengthy process and by the time the property was purchased, I was busy doing other things, so I did not have the time to engage the builders to do the work in the loft for the two bedrooms.

I have given you these examples because you can be obsessed with trying to get something for the sake of trying to get it, and then when you get it you realise that you do not have the time or resources to complete the task. And this is what both property deals came to. So, in business just because you can do something, and just because you can fight your way through the complexities to do it, there is no point in doing it, if you cannot complete the task, just to prove to yourself or anyone else that you can.

So, the moral of this story is, what you do in one area you can probably do in another. The effort it takes to get a profit on a £250,000 property, that you can work on and turn around, does not take any more effort than if the property that you are purchasing is £500,000. The only difference is us limiting ourselves.

The process of obtaining a mortgage on a property as a self-employed person, is quite different to that of an employed person. As an employed person you would usually need to confirm your employment, by giving authorisation to the mortgage company to contact your employer for a reference. The reference would confirm that your employment is permanent, and that your earnings are consistent, so the mortgage company would check that your earnings would be enough to repay the mortgage comfortably. You can usually borrow three, four and even five times your income, depending on the criteria set out by the bank or building society.

As a self-employed person, you would usually be required to have been trading for at least three years. Your accounts would need to be certified by an accountant, and the income multiples would normally be based on 'x' amount times of profit. So, as you can see, it is usually more difficult to get a mortgage as a self-employed person, than a person in regular employment.

Chapter 13
Seville Lodge

Prior to the property crash in the eighties, I was flying high, and everything was going smoothly. I was buying properties, renting out properties, running bed and breakfasts, a mother and baby hostel, money was coming in and everything was fine. I was driving around in my prestige car, and I thought 'life doesn't get much better than this!'

However, I soon realised that due to market forces, there are certain things we cannot control as businesspeople. In my case it was the economy, the property market took a downturn, and I did not know what to do.

This was the first time I came across an area in business where I was completely shocked. The local authority also changed the rules, so where we used to have people in bed and breakfast until they were housed, the legislation changed so that people on benefits could only stay in a bed and breakfast for four weeks at a time.

Many things changed so quickly that I started running around like a headless chicken, but a lot of this was because I did not plan for a downturn. I just felt that if I kept doing what I was doing, then things would just get better; the properties would always be rented out, people would always be paying their rent, and the prices of the properties would continue to grow.

However, by the early nineties I was struggling. I had borrowed money and paid high interest rates. I saw that I was unable to fill the rooms in the same way I used to be able to. I also realised property market prices were going down, instead of going up, so I had to change my direction. I sold two of the larger properties, that I had gotten planning permission on to turn into flats, because I did not have the money to do the conversions myself.

I sold the properties to mitigate my losses, and then I had to sell a further four properties as they were not making a profit. So, after flying high through the eighties as a young man, now into the nineties and not so young anymore, I did not really know the direction I would be taking.

Do not get me wrong, being in business is good, planning what you are doing is good, marketing and market research is good; but I do not want to give anyone the impression that if you keep doing what you are doing, it keeps going well. Market forces are out of your control and can have a devastating impact on what you are doing.

Sometimes, it does not have to be market forces, it could be to do with relationships, illness, or it could be anything else. Be aware, and always try to prepare yourself for doing something different if what you are doing is not going as well as you thought it would.

After my properties sold. I got involved in the care industry, which my parents were already involved in, and started working my way back up.

Over 30 years ago, my mother and father started a company called *Seville Lodge*. They purchased a bungalow in Wokingham and turned it into a residential care home for the elderly. My mother, having previously been a nurse, had all the necessary skills to manage it. She recruited staff and trained them to be carers, in their 13-bed care home.

Many of the bedrooms were ensuite, and the bungalow had a large garden. After running this for many years, my siblings and I were visiting the home often and meeting the residents. My father sadly passed away and the time came where my mother wanted to take a back seat, so two of my sisters and I, decided to expand Seville Lodge, and we created a company called Seville Care Homes.

Along with Seville Lodge, we purchased Magnolia Lodge, and Hamilton House, two large properties that also had clients. Magnolia Lodge, and Hamilton House, were for people with learning and physical disabilities, whereas Seville Lodge was for the elderly.

One of the tips we took from my mother, in terms of her very caring nature, was to ensure that the clients would go on outings. They would celebrate birthdays with family visits and have loads of balloons at the property. Sometimes, we would have garden parties, and day outings, as well as encourage family and friends to visit.

There would be bingo, and board games played, and we would continue to ensure that the clients really had the best treatment. We were able to adapt our training, our own skills, and recruit other members of staff with further skills to manage Magnolia Lodge, and Hamilton House. One of us, either myself or one of my sisters, would be the lead person at each of the properties.

One day, I remember receiving a fancy letter through the mail, and this letter was addressed to a resident at Seville Lodge. It was a letter from the Queen, wishing the resident a happy 100th birthday.

If I were not involved in health and social care, I would have never known that the Queen writes to you when you reach the grand age of one hundred. The lady was over the moon, and it lifted everyone's spirit; the fact that the Queen had written to a resident.

We kept these properties for some years, until a housing company offered us more money than Seville Lodge was worth. This company had already secured purchasing both properties to the left and right of ours.

At the time, my mother was looking to retire early, so my sisters and I continued to run Magnolia Lodge and Hamilton House as a part of Seville Care Homes, until both properties became subject of a takeover by a large national healthcare company.

My sisters and I decided to go our separate ways until I returned to the care industry some years later.

Chapter 14
Mentee to Mentor

I had a mentor who was a very unlikely mentor and came about purely by accident. There was a man around town by the name of Mac, that many people knew, and he was involved in purchasing property, and letting out those properties to individual people, on a bed and breakfast basis.

He used to eat regularly at a café in the town centre, and many of us would go there to meet, and at the same time have something to eat. The café is still running all these years later.

I was 18 years old at the time, and I had fortunately purchased a house, which I then let out to tenants. I let out three bedrooms, and the room downstairs, so there were four rooms let, in addition to a living room, kitchen, and bathroom.

One day we got talking, and he said to me 'have you thought of buying another property and joining in with me? I have properties, but they are all full and there is a waiting list of people, so if you purchased a property or two, I could put people in them on a bed and breakfast basis, which I'll manage, and you can pay me a small management fee.'

From the property I let out, I saved money from the rent I received, for a deposit on another house. I got a mortgage and purchased another property when I was 20 years old, purchased another when I was 21 years old, and then I put all three properties into his company. The properties were filled with tenants and we shared responsibility for the maintenance and bed and breakfast service.

This went on for a few years; he filled my properties, and in return I worked for him. I helped with his business, by managing the maintenance and tenant aspects of the business.

I soon realised that I was being unconsciously mentored by this businessman, and I felt it was my duty to do the same for others. It is important for us to acknowledge those who have inspired us and helped us to believe that whatever we put our minds to, and by working hard enough we can achieve.

A few years later, I made some enquiries into a local mentoring scheme, as I felt I was now ready to become a mentor. I met with the manager of Reading Education and Business Partnership, which ran a local scheme set up by the local authority. We were interviewed, and once selected, we were trained to develop our skills as mentors, which included listening skills. The role was a voluntary position, so we did not get paid for it.

I thought it was a very fulfilling role for both parties, because being a mentor was my way of giving back to the community, and my mentee felt he was receiving support over and above what he was getting at school, and from other support services that his school offered. The young man I mentored was in a secondary school, he was a very polite young man, always dressed well, and well mannered.

What I found interesting when we got paired up by the organisation, was that I was given the impression that the mentoring scheme was really for young people who did not engage well at school, and who the school feared would not engage well outside of school in the real world. The mentoring scheme went well and at the end of it there were certificates for the young people, and for the successful mentors.

Over ten years after completing the mentoring scheme, I was walking down a road and I bumped into the young man that I had mentored. Jimmy shook my hand and gave me a manly embrace, and I was really chuffed. He told me he had his own driving school. He gave me his number, and when my nephews and nieces were looking to start their driving lessons, I would recommend them and many others to him. Many of them passed their driving tests being taught by the young man. The incredible thing about that was that we bumped into one another by pure accident.

I covered this success story in my magazine a couple of years later, and he mentioned me being his mentor and that I had inspired him to start his own business. I think that is what being someone's mentor is, you get to spend time with someone and share experiences with them, and try to point them in the right direction, whilst letting them know that you care.

When you put it all together, seeing a young person come through, and see them being successful and having their own business; it makes it all worthwhile and I am grateful for the scheme, for helping me to become a mentor. I am really pleased I managed to inspire the young man to become successful.

A few years later, I was voted the chair of an independent charitable organisation called Reading Refocus. This was a mentoring organisation that worked primarily with schools. The young people were chosen because their teachers felt they could benefit from mentoring support, and the organisation I chaired would train people from the local community to become mentors, to support these young people.

Part of the agreement was that they would see the young people once a week, and monitor the progress set against certain milestones.

The mentors were carefully chosen by our organisation, and the mentees were chosen by the school. As with many voluntary organisations we were dependent on external funding.

After several years of some particularly good work, the organisation's funding was severely cut, and the organisation was forced to minimise its services and move premises. This meant that we had to change the way we did things.

I felt that it was the right time to step down after three years of service, so I handed in my resignation, to focus on my business activities.

Chapter 15
Capital Direct

Following my involvement in the property market, I gained a great deal of knowledge about funding, and financing properties. I also learnt a lot about mortgages, so for me to become a Financial Advisor, was a natural progression, dealing with mortgages, and insurance products.

To start, you had to enrol on a financial regulatory course for one week. During that course, you would learn about the legal aspects, and different financial products, then at the end of the week you would take a test, and if you passed you could move onto the next steps, of learning the practical and sales aspects, of becoming a Financial Advisor.

I was not an independent financial advisor; I was tied to a company called CCL Financial Services. This meant that I could only offer financial products that they provided. Payment to me was via commission.

Even though I was self-employed, I was allocated a pot of money by CCL Financial Services. For example, you would have a pot of £3,000 that you could use, so it was like an overdraft that the company gave you, which meant that the first couple of months, I could earn, even if I did not have any commission.

For the first two months after completing my course, I was the highest earner in terms of commission. It was not directly from mortgages; most of it, in fact was from other products being sold by me, such as life insurance, and pensions.

Being from quite a large family, and having many friends, the obvious thing for me to do, was convince my friends and family to take out insurances or financial services from me, so that I could collect the commission.

The upside of this work was that at the end of each month, I would get paid my commission, but the downside was that if the insurance, or whatever I had signed my clients up for, was cancelled within a year, I would have to forfeit that same commission. So, in effect I had to sign up people that really wanted the products, rather than friends and family, that wanted to help me earn money.

The industry was good, and I was continually learning, and going on courses about sales and customer service. I would also learn a script, usually given to us on an A4 sheet of paper, to sell the insurance, or other products, and I would remember that script, and quote it word for word.

Working in the financial services industry was interesting, as I would meet all different types of people, but the downside for me was that I had to dress smart every day, which meant wearing a suit, shirt, and tie. If there is one thing that gets to me, it is putting on a tie, as it makes me feel like I am choking. So, despite how much I enjoyed the financial services industry, I could not continue with a job that expected me to wear a tie every day.

Most of what I was doing, was selling. In business, most of the time, you are selling either products or services. After a while, I cut my ties with CCL.

Once I left, I went fully independent as a Financial Broker, where I was brokering deals at the higher end of prestige motor car finance.

Capital Direct was a finance brokerage, that I started up, because I had a strong interest in cars. Capital Direct was a brokerage that used to broker finance deals for people to buy cars, normally prestige cars.

We put together some marketing; advertised in a local newspaper, handed out flyers and leaflets and the rest was by word of mouth. People would look for a car at a garage and rather than taking advice from the people who worked there, in terms of them buying a car and getting the finance from the garage, they would speak to me. It could be straight forward to get finance for people to purchase their car without any razzmatazz salesperson.

Capital Direct rented an office, and clients would call the office and all the information they gave us would go on a proposal form. Some clients would complete the form themselves, by email.

We would then require their identification, which we would have to see physically, and we would photocopy it along with other ID documents, such as passport, driving licence, proof of address, and utility bills with the client's name on them. All the identification documents would have to be at the same address. Once the finance company were sent the details from us, they would do the credit checks, employment checks and so on.

The finance company would also check that the vehicle is not currently on finance, or been in an accident, or stolen and sold. If the vehicle was more than three years old, the finance company would also check that it had a valid MOT and so on. Once all that had all been checked out, the finance company would then advance a high percentage of the vehicle price, normally 90%, and the client would put the remaining 10%.

The finance company would send documents to the garage that the client would then sign, and they could then drive away the vehicle, as they would have signed that they agreed to pay a monthly payment for that vehicle. The client would get copies of the signed documents, sent to them directly.

Capital Direct, would then receive a commission from the finance company, that would be paid one month after the vehicle was delivered.

If the vehicle is paid for every month, the client will own it after 3-4 years, depending on how long the hire purchase agreement was signed for. Sometimes, people would decide to borrow some money from elsewhere, and pay it off before the end of the term or sell the vehicle before the term ends and settle the finance.

If things did not go so well, and the purchaser did not pay all the payments, the finance company would take some action, and make an order to take them to court, or sometimes collect the vehicle by repossessing it, and then it would be back in the finance company's hands. The downside for the customer, is that it is usually sold at an auction, and the finance company will roll up all unpaid interest, and then take them to court for that amount. So, my advice is, make sure you can afford it and pay, and make sure you do so, before it gets more expensive with late payment fees etc. Once we received the commission for the vehicle, that was basically the end of our relationship with the vehicle and the customer. However, the customer would end up having an ongoing relationship with the finance company, until the end of the term on the agreement.

Capital Direct also offered insurance options to customers against possible loss of income. This could cover up to a year of repayments whilst the customer was unemployed.

The advantage of finance is that you could have the vehicle now, rather than later, and you would be paying the same payments every month. We had favourable deals for our own vehicles, and they were financed through the same company that we used for vehicles found by the customer, until they got bought out by a larger company, and the brokers were no longer required.

Chapter 16

Train the Trainer

Training professionals can come in many forms; however, I never saw myself as a 'trainer'. If I ever did, I would not have considered myself being involved in the training of police officers, in community relations.

Over the years, there has been several inquiries into policing in the UK, and after each inquiry, a report is produced and recommendations are made, which are outcome focused.

The Home Office is the government department that is responsible for policing in the UK. The Equalities and Human Rights Commission (EHRC) has been set up to ensure that all government organisations act within the equality law.

Many years ago, the police were referred to as a 'police force', but I now understand they prefer to be referred to as the 'police service'. More recently the police service has focused on making themselves more representative, so that they reflect the communities they serve.

The police have tried to attract more people from the Black, Asian, and Minority Ethnic (BAME) communities, women, and people from the lesbian, gay, bisexual, and transgender (LGBTQ) communities. Most of the focus on advertising has been to attract people from diverse communities, and although there has been some progress, it seems it is not at a level that the police, or indeed the government, or the community, feel it should be.

In my opinion, one of the most difficult jobs in this country is to be a police officer. The main reason, I think, is because most of the interactions that the police have with the public are confrontational, and this is the problem.

Confrontational interaction is perceived to be negative. One example is, if someone calls the police because they have been a victim of crime, they expect results. If there are no immediate results, they may become angry with the police. If the police were to make an arrest, then the perpetrator would become angry with the police. So, it seems on many occasions, the police are damned if they do, and damned if they don't.

Sometimes, police get a hard time, whilst at other times they get praised. However, when my friends and I were growing up, we never viewed being a police officer as a good career choice, and that is what I think needs to change.

I think that there are some young people in the community, who should be encouraged to take up a career within the police service. There is a lot of training provided, and when you do get it right, which I am sure most of the time they do, there is a lot of job satisfaction.

After one of the many community meetings I attended some years ago, a community representative approached me, and asked if I would be interested in training police trainers, as a part of their promotion. The people receiving the training would be police officers, that are being promoted to higher ranks, and part of the training was about community relations.

With my self-employed hat on, I decided to get involved with some freelance work and become a sub-contractor. The organisation that had the contract was recruiting people that they could appoint, to train the police officers, or in this case the police trainers.

I embarked upon the community trainer programme, and I was involved with police training for a couple of years at Bramshill, Sulhampstead, and Harrogate Police Training Colleges.

The training that we were involved in varied, sometimes it would be for a whole day, and at other times it would be for two, or three days, so we would stay overnight at the venue. There were different set ups when we got there. Sometimes we would speak with the police trainers one to one, at other times there would be groups of us, including police officers, who would ask questions, and put forward scenarios, it was a real eye opener.

Sometimes, during the training, there would be gasps from the police, if we touched on a subject that was sensitive for them. Overall, even though we were being paid for our time, and they were very much interactive sessions, I felt I met some wonderful people.

During the training sessions, we would tackle real life subjects, and at other times we would do some role plays. There were situations, where police officers would storm off out of the group, because they would become angry, and there were a couple of police officers that shouted during the training, sometimes out of frustration.

There was also a lot of laughter, and there were some good people involved in the training. We were involved in group work and presentations, and we would also get feedback, and there would be handouts at the end of each session.

Some senior police officers invited me to Northern Ireland, and some other faraway places, but considering the travelling involved, I did not take up the invitations.

It was a really good experience, and although we were the trainers, I learnt a lot about policing, about the culture of policing, and I was able to share some of my experiences, and some of the experiences of the peers that I grew up with. We were able to give a grass roots element to the police and community relations training.

I really hope that the feeling we got at the end of the sessions, including some of the feedback, and the messages that came through, was that the police officers, even those who found it quite difficult to accept examples that were given, felt at the end that it was a positive experience that worked for the betterment of society.

Issue 2 November 2001
Thames Valley Edition

URBANnews

Covering African, Caribbean & Asian Community Lifestyle, Culture & Entertainment

Win "Invincible"
MICHAEL JACKSON

Who Am I?
BEVERLEY KNIGHT

Career Guide
PACKED WITH JOBS & ADVICE

Matthew Syed meets with Prime minister, Tony Blair.

To the right, Syed in Table Tennis action.

Commonwealth champion to local council in sixty days

Matthew Syed, aged 30 and originally from Reading, is the current British and Commonwealth Table Tennis champion. Currently no.63 in the world and having reached a peak of no.24, the vastly experienced Syed, is England's highest world ranked player. He plays a spectacular, long-range defensive game and currently is probably the greatest retriever of the ball in the sport. A feature writer for *The Times*, a TV commentator on SKY, and possessing a first class degree in Politics, Philosophy and Economics, the multi-faceted Syed was the Labour Party's prospective candidate for the parliamentary constituency of Wokingham (John Redwood's seat).

Matthew has one big ambition left in table tennis, "With the Commonwealth Games coming to Manchester in 2002 and table tennis joining the Games for the first time, my major target must be to win a record 4th Commonwealth men's singles title".

With his best playing days probably behind him, what will his table tennis

involvement be after the Games? "I will have to think very carefully and decide whether to carry on playing. The issue will be more a motivational rather than a physical one." If he gave up table tennis, what other career might he pursue? He will take stock of his recent experience fighting for Labour in the General Election, before deciding whether to stand again. "I also enjoy writing and commentating on TV very much and possibly might go more into that. But I have no firm plans."

The General Election very nearly prevented Syed from his (successful) defence of the Commonwealth men's singles title in New Delhi in April this year, achieved in an epic, cliffhanging final with India's top player Chetan Baboor, during which he held 7 match points, and saved 3 match points, before scraping through 28-26 in the fifth game. Syed explains, "Had the Election gone ahead on the expected date of May 3rd, then I would not have **(Continues on page 30)**

(Continues on page 30)

Chapter 17
Urban News

Urban News started off as a concept that came from an annual report I developed, whilst I was Chair of Reading Community Carnival, for its 21st anniversary. The Carnival report I produced was in full colour, and we had some advertisements from small local businesses to fund the production of the report. After the success of the Carnival report, I thought our community can use a magazine as a way of communicating positive stories and celebrating role models. A few years later, I developed 'Urban News', a free monthly magazine, and we got to a stage where we were producing magazines for many thousands of readers each month.

I was knowledgeable on how the local authorities, and the Arts Council work, and their statutory responsibility to all communities, so we approached those organisations to advertise their services. We would advertise many small community groups free of charge, because we knew paying for advertising was difficult for them.

In terms of how the magazine looked visually, it was inspired by 'Hello magazine', so it was slightly larger than A4 and very colourful. The difference was that whereas 'Hello' magazine was all about celebrities, we were pretty much a magazine about the community.

I was funding the magazine to produce 20,000 copies per month. Due to the escalated costs of the production, reduced public sector funds, and no loans or overdraft it was a struggle to continue. The public sector had been going through financial cuts, and as a part of those cuts, advertising, especially in small magazines like ours, was the first to go.

In the magazine, we would interview and profile volunteers, charity workers, and celebrities, who wanted to talk about their charitable work. The magazine was well received, and because of that, I was interviewed on the radio, and invited to many high-profile events.

The magazine got me invited to many places such as the MOBO Awards, and Screen Nation Awards in London.

We went to events in top hotels in London. The biggest event was a Mandela dinner, when Nelson Mandela came to unveil a statue of himself in London. There was a dinner in his honour the night before, however he was not feeling well, so some of his grandchildren came, and they addressed the audience on his behalf. The audience was like a list of who's who, it was excellent, and everyone was friendly.

I was invited to the Houses of Parliament to interview politicians, on other occasions I interviewed actors, musicians, community activists, Olympians, and comedians. You name it, we had access to do the interviews.

We would also get sent different CD's from record companies to review, and because of Urban News' community impact we won a millennium award.

For far too long, we have been leaving the documenting of our voluntary community work to the mass media, and as we all know, the mass media are ready to jump on stories about us when we get it wrong, but hardly recognise when we get it right.

That is why I felt it was important to have a way of communicating the fantastic work of the voluntary community sector through the magazine, and Urban News did that very effectively. Our full colour magazine displayed community work and put a voluntary sector magazine on par with the major mass market magazines. Those magazines had millions of pounds of backing and could call upon well-known celebrities to grace their front covers and inside pages.

We believe that there are people out there, who are interested in things that may not be so glamorous but are more meaningful, and things that may not be so celebrity driven but purposeful. We were able to highlight that by hooking up with the most amazing individuals.

The other thing we found, was that it is all well and good to label groups as 'hard to reach', but those so-called groups are only hard to reach by the people who are happy to put that label onto them.

The so-called 'hard to reach' groups, are sometimes the easiest to reach. We found that those groups have been very willing to share their stories. The fact that people, in their own time and for no money, would put together some of the community groups, and support so many voluntary groups doing good work, has always amazed me.

If we can give those people the same kind of multi-colour, multi-faceted, high resolution photos, and cover their story in their own words, then that is what it is all about. That is why we do what we do in our magazine. There is no way that we would believe that a celebrity is more important, simply because they are a celebrity.

Many people that do voluntary community work, are just as important as any celebrity. They do not do it for fame and fortune, they dedicate themselves to voluntary community work, in their own personal time. Some people continue for many years without any real recognition, without the award ceremony, and without the double page spread.

Many voluntary community people do what they do quite privately, and they do what they do because they want some of the people in need, to benefit from what they do. Urban News was always wanting to celebrate those unrecognised individuals, doing such magnanimous things.

2004 was the end of my stint in magazine publishing, due to escalating costs, and the lack of advertising, it came to a time where the magazine had to be shelved.

Every now and then, I felt an itch to publish another magazine, and around 2012, I started putting together plans to relaunch another community magazine. This time it was going to be quarterly, not monthly, and the magazine would be called 'Today'.

Today Magazine was really a continuation of Urban News, however the significant difference was, that rather than being a larger than A4 size, which sometimes made it difficult for people to carry, and put in their handbags or laptop cases, this one was A4, and did what Urban News did.

Today Magazine featured similar front cover page stories and articles, and there was never a shortage of such articles or community people to interview, including some high-profile people, such as the local mayor. We continued with sharing good news stories and articles about the community. This included the head of a national children's charity, local and national charities, the director of our local football club, a local film director, a local playwright, actors, a boxing champion, a leading martial arts club, dancers, community members, and the list goes on.

Chapter 18
The Big Debate

When I was 18, a friend of mine called Welch, said to me 'come along to this community meeting, you might find it interesting'. I went to the meeting and I was hooked. The most amazing thing about it was the intelligence and wisdom of the committee members that were involved in this ground-breaking community group.

I found it mesmerising, so I went to a few meetings, and eventually I joined as a committee member. That really kicked off my community work, and the various community organisations that I have been involved with.

The great thing about community work, is that you do it out of love for the community. You do not do it for money, as you do not get paid. I have been involved with many organisations through the years, and even as a businessperson the experience is invaluable. I have gained new skills, knowledge and general know how from being involved in community organisations.

In or around 2003, I decided to form a community organisation. I set up an organisation called Urban UK Network, and it was for people within the urban community, mainly towns and cities. I wanted to do something different. I continued being involved in other organisations too, but I wanted to start one that could communicate with the community, a little bit more effectively than I felt the current organisations were doing. The community would be able to have a forum to speak directly to the decision makers, especially the people involved within the local authority.

We contacted the local authority and explained that we have the expertise, knowledge, and experience to be able to attract some of the people, they want to attract. We know that the council are concerned as a local authority, that the services they fund and deliver, are not reaching all communities, and we believe that in terms of the way we would promote events, we would really be able to cement a partnership with the council.

Many different groups, that could be considered minority groups, had issues. We contacted key individuals within those organisations and asked them to forward the information to their own contacts.

Urban UK Network would then hold a forum, once, or sometimes twice a year, with like-minded people, who would be invited into the audience. I would chair that forum. The audience would be community people. The panel would be made up of local authority officers, politicians, and representatives from the health service, social services, police, and so on.

We would email businesspeople and ask them if they would be willing to sit on a panel, and answer questions from the local community. It was received well, and we decided that we will call this event *'The Big Debate'*. There could be several topics on the agenda; from the public sector, private sector, newspaper, TV, charitable, voluntary and community sectors, where people would have the freedom to come and debate.

This work is all a part of my commitment to promoting dialogue between the community and representatives of the authorities, and mostly the politicians. I have held The Big Debate since around 2009. It is normally held in the Council Chamber at the local council offices, or at a community centre.

Whilst being involved in business or community activities, events and organisations, people continue to ask me to say some of the things that they want to say, or to question the Chief Executives, or elected representatives at meetings, that is why I decided to start 'The Big Debate'. They ask me, because they want to know about, why this is this way, and why that is that way, but they do not know how, or where, they can ask their questions. On one hand, you have the community asking people like myself questions to take to the powers to be, and on the other hand, you have the so-called powers, or politicians, saying that they are finding a lot of members from community groups that they would like to have better dialogue with.

I am a fan of BBC's 'Question Time' programme, where four or five panellists sit with the Chairperson. The panellists are normally politicians, and sometimes newspaper editors, authors, businesspeople, journalists, and such, and I felt that we could do this on a community level.

Each year, the local authority has kindly allowed us to use their venue, and all we must do is pick a panel of our choice and put out the word. The panel normally consists of leaders of the main local political parties i.e. Conservative, Labour, Liberal Democrats, and Green Party. Sometimes we have business leaders, other politicians, community activists, police officers, charity, and community representatives. The debate normally lasts approximately two hours during an evening.

The event has been continuously well supported over the years, and after each debate, we have spoken to people that have been involved, whether as part of the audience, or by asking questions. People have always said they have had an incredibly positive experience from the event.

The local media has also been involved, by reporting on The Big Debate, sometimes even advertising that it is going to be on. The local radio has also covered the debate in the same way.

I have always been of the impression that it is not so much what the politicians, the town, or the country can do for us, but sometimes it is about what we can do for them. The community will get together and sometimes in greater numbers, if they perceive that a member of the community has put on the event, irrespective of who is on the panel. Sometimes, they will come together more than if it was the same event being run by any of the agencies that we have had as panellists.

Attendees would give us their contact details, so they can be notified for future events. They would also pick up a slip that would be ready for them at the beginning of the event as they enter. They would write down their questions, and hold onto the slip, raise their hands during the question and answer session, and read their question from the slip.

Alternatively, they would hand the slip to me, or one of us on the panel, and ask us to ask their question on their behalf. The slips were highly effective, some of the issues were very emotive, some of them were sad, some of them were about children, some of them were about adults, schools, jobs, lack of housing provision etc. We really did get down to some meaningful discussions. We also had feedback forms that we would ask people to fill out and these would help us in selecting the panel or following up with our panel after an event.

It has been a great experience, and long may it continue!

Chapter 19
Nesta Care

I was involved in the care industry earlier in my business life. Then, I went back into the care business when I thought the climate was right.

Nesta Care was a company I set up to care for vulnerable adults with disabilities, in their own homes. On occasions, we would provide accommodation with care staff, and this is what is called 'Supported Living'. We recruited staff that we would then train as carers. These carers would go into people's houses and provide care for them.

Part of setting up a care business, whether you have previously been involved in the industry or not, is proving to the local authorities that you are a fit and proper person and the people you employ are competent to work with vulnerable people too. There is a whole recruitment and selection process and these processes must be followed diligently. If you are caring for clients where the local authority is paying for their care, that care must be delivered in line with what the local authorities and Care Quality Commission (CQC) deem appropriate, so due diligence must be carried out.

Whilst we were running Nesta Care we worked with many professionals who would be dealing with the clients. We dealt with care managers, occupational therapists, GP's, psychologists, psychiatrists, nurses, and solicitors.

It is said in marketing speak, that the best people to market to, are people that you have done business with before, or those that are your current customers. This not only works in terms of marketing to your customers; I also think that it works in terms of businesses you have been involved with. If you have been involved in a business before, then it is quite straightforward to get involved with that type of business again. In fact, I have done that on a few occasions.

To get started, you could contact a local authority, and ask them for their criteria in terms of what you will need to be that fit and proper person to provide care. The process took us about a year to gain full registration. In order to provide personal care, we needed a Registered Manager, who had to have a disclosure and barring service (DBS) check, provide their full employment history with no gaps unaccounted for, and then be interviewed by a CQC representative.

In terms of recruitment, you must investigate and ensure you have every single employee's identification documents, including address verification, and photo ID. The criteria is very strict, so a mobile phone bill is not acceptable as proof of address, it has to be a utility bill (gas, electric or a water bill), council tax bill, landline telephone bill or a credit card bill, bank or mortgage statement.

Candidates are then interviewed, and you must be able to provide proof that the interview was conducted correctly. All the information you need for a CQC registration, and about compliance, is available on the Care Quality Commission website. It is a process that is lengthy, but it does mean that you have fit and proper personnel in your employment to send out to a client's home to support them.

The support provided to clients would be things such as personal care, which includes toileting and bathing, helping clients get dressed, ordering and administering medication, shopping, and cooking etc.

After the first month of service, the employee would receive a supervision meeting with a manager, this would happen monthly for the first three months of the proba-tionary period. Following a successful probationary period, the employee would be supervised every three months. Staff would have a 360-degree appraisal annu-ally, which is an appraisal that takes into consideration speaking to social workers, clients and their families, and managers. All the information received is put together and an independent person would come in and perform the appraisal to see how that staff member is doing. It really is an in-depth procedure.

As I am writing this book, the care industry is going through some changes, the main change being that there is less money available to authorities to pay for care packages. Many of the staff are not highly qualified and the care industry is known for paying minimum wage. When you pay a low wage, you do not always get the best out of your employees. Another aspect is the Care Quality Commission (CQC) inspections, where some larger and smaller homes do not have particularly good reports.

We need the government to look at the care industry. With the advent of the living wage being introduced, the minimum wage being increased, and the introduction of the pension scheme that we all must sign up to, it is becoming increasingly difficult for small companies to survive in the care industry, and it may be only the multi-million-pound corporations that are going to be able to survive. I am not sure that it is the best way forward, because some of these large companies are in business mainly to please their shareholders, they are profit driven. These corporations are getting marked down a lot, regarding the quality of care they are providing to vulnerable people. This is very much on the agenda in the news, and it is going to be interesting to see over the next few months and years, how all of what is happening now shapes the care industry of the future.

It is not that I do not have bad days, sometimes in business I do have bad days, but more often I have good days. With so many more good days than bad days, and because I am cut from a certain cloth, I would say that being in the caring sector is a job well worth doing.

Chapter 20
Avoiding Naysayers

I am not sure if you can write a book about being self-employed, or about running your own business, without including the issue of '*naysayers*'.

As humans, we always seem to look to find someone around us that we know we can depend on to use as a sounding board; it could be family or friends, that we ask what they think of an idea. Within that, you sometimes get naysayers. It is not that I think everyone you talk to must say 'it's a great idea', but the whole issue around naysayers, is that every idea is not a good idea to them. They say things like, 'if it were so good someone else would have thought of it', or, 'there you go again dreaming up ideas that are not going to work'. That is what naysayers seem to say, and none of that negative energy helps. In fact, that negative energy pulls you down, because it is quite strong.

Although some of these naysayers have a lot of energy, they seem to have most of it directed towards being negative. I find when they are criticising an idea, if you then try to explain to them why you think that idea might work, they go into second gear regarding their negativity, by saying you are being unrealistic, and that they are being realistic. It can weigh you down.

Sometimes, things do not work, and if they do not work and the naysayers find out that it did not work, they put a lot of positive energy into telling you how right they were, 'see I told you it wouldn't work, and it didn't work'.

The best thing to do, is to surround yourself with people, who give you constructive criticism. So, they look at your idea and say, 'it's a good idea, have you considered this, or have you considered that'. They can really give you a positive spin, so that you can look at the idea, and consider it from different angles, or consider aspects of it that you had not considered before.

Also, you may come across people who blame everyone for anything that has happened to them, that might have been negative. They tend to not take responsibility themselves. Those people are complainers, they do not equate anything they have failed at, to anything they have done, it is always someone else's fault. This is another thing that can pull you down. If you have people like that around you, you should probably be drawn away from them.

You may see something on the news, highlighting conflicts, and wars. Again, and again, doom, gloom, and negativity. But there are some people that say everything is bad, everything is going to lead to the end of the world. If you make a success of your project, you will get the naysayer saying that you are only successful because of something someone else has put into it, and not because of your own efforts. I must emphasise, that there are circumstances that are negative, where some bad things do happen, however there are also many circumstances, where good things happen.

That is the whole thing about naysayers, you must try not to be too close to them for too long. That negative energy can sometimes consume you, and have you doubting yourself, because we are only human, and we take on board lots of things people say, especially those closest to us. Those people are not conducive to working for you, because you must be supported by positivity in every way, shape, and form. Be aware in terms of the people around you, and how they may impact upon you. Bear in mind, that there are positive people that you can connect to, and who can support your ideas.

We have spoken about naysayers you know that you have around you. Now let us look at naysayers who have been in business or self-employed. Despite them having that attitude they went into business, but the negativity still got to them in the end.

I have heard failed business people say: -

- It was because of my business partner that my business failed because they were doing things I did not know about.
- It was my staff, as they were not committed, and they did not do the work they were brought on board to do, so the business eventually folded.

- It was the accountant, that did not do the accounts correctly, and they just messed up, so the business went under.
- It was my husband that did not support me when I was at home, and basically got in the way of my all ideas, and scuppered my dreams, so that the business then failed.
- It was my colour that stopped people wanting to do business with me.
- It was my legal advisor, and when I went to ask for advice about my business, they led me in the wrong direction.
- It was my brother, who kept asking questions about what I was doing, and rather than supporting me, he wouldn't, and he borrowed loads of money from me that he couldn't pay back, so I couldn't put it back in the business, so the business failed.
- It was my mother in law that made my business fail, because she never liked me, so she turned my family against me, and then my wife started being negative about the business, not supporting me.
- It was the weather, because my business was weather dependant, and because it continued to rain throughout the year, it wrecked my idea, and the business folded.
- It was my suppliers, they did not supply the equipment on time, and I had already paid upfront, and then had to pay customers back their money, so my business failed.

Now, the key to all of what I have said, is that at no time are these people acknowledging that the one unique factor there is them. No, it cannot possibly be them, it must be every single other person, or the situation. If you are like that, or see yourself becoming like that, and you can bring it back to you, and you can take full responsibility for what happens, this just might be your saving grace.

By avoiding naysayers, you save yourself a lot of time and energy. You can use that saved time to concentrate on other areas of your business, such as marketing.

Chapter 21
Market Research

How will you know your product or service is required, the numbers of people interested, where, when, and how to get in touch with them? You must carry out some *market research*.

Many of us who start a business, automatically feel there are customers that want our product or service. However, there are ways of testing this. The best way to start, is with people you know, send them a text, email, or message on social media. Ask them how much of your product/service they would require and chase them up for answers. Do not forget that most people are busy, and you are not their number one priority; so, send reminders, and keep on, until you get an answer. If all else fails, give them a phone call.

This information or feedback will be your survey, that you use as market research. You can use the same approach to consider your pricing, and other aspects of your business.

Starting a business with no market research, is like watering soil without a seed, and expecting a flower to grow.

Let's imagine that you are quite handy with a paint brush, and you decide to start your own painting and decorating company, as you have had enough of being pushed around at work. Before you leave your job, you need to develop enough continuous work, to replace your full-time income, and you decide to work weekends until you can secure a replacement income.

You should first contact people you know, and hand out leaflets, or business cards. Some business cards can still be printed free of charge if you carry the printing company's name and contact details on them. Leaflets can be typed on A4 paper and cut into four. Ten of those and you have forty leaflets with your name and mobile number on. Remember to start with the people you know, follow your market research principle, and hey presto, you have put your market research into action.

Another example is, that you are quite handy at knitting; you have a young baby at home, and you would like to use the time when your baby is asleep to make some money. You decide to knit baby clothes and collect baby clothes you no longer want and sell them, for example on eBay. You could join a mother and toddler club, contact all your friends that either already have babies, or children that have grown up, but still have bags of baby clothes they no longer need. Using this market research strategy, you can build your own affordable supply base.

Then you can purchase a domain name, and a website template, for an affordable amount of money. Take photos of your products with your mobile phone and upload them onto your website. The order comes in and the client pays using one of the many applications that allow people to pay through your website. You wrap the goods, and post them to your clients, whilst you and your baby are out for a stroll. The money is paid through your website and goes straight into your bank account. How cool is that? All the methods and steps mentioned in this book on how to start/run a business can be found on the internet by carrying out searches.

We need to keep in mind, that from the outside things look different, to how the people who are on the inside see things.

In terms of family life, or in terms of business, someone might say something, and you think, why do they see things like that. For example, if you stand two inches away from a large oak tree, and you look at it, you will see the creases in the bark and the fine detail, but if you then stand ten or twenty feet away, you can see the whole tree, its leaves, and its branches.

Also, there are different cultures and different languages that may do the same thing, getting slightly different results. If you are familiar doing something one way, and you see someone doing it another way, you may think that is not the way to do it, 'the correct way to do it is the way I do it', but both may be correct as long as you both get the best results.

For example, one business may decide to invoice for a job, and on the invoice put cheque payable to 'your name or the company'. Another business may provide the invoice, and include their bank details on it, and state, 'please transfer directly to this bank account', providing payment terms. If we could look at examples of things that work, and if we can speak to people who have had proof of success in their field, or similar fields of what we want to do, then that is a good start.

I would not advise someone to speak to a plumber, who is a specialist in plumbing, and ask them for details about how to do electrical work. I would suggest you speak to an electrician for that. I think that analogy goes across all sectors; do not ask a landscape gardener to help you solve the problem with your car, and so on.

People go to their bank managers and ask them for business advice. While the bank manager, manages a bank, a business adviser, advises businesses. Some of the peoples' skills sets do cut across into different areas; although an accountant deals with accounts, but because they are around money and finance, accountants can also offer financial advice.

Also, when you are looking to move forward, do not just take the advice of one person and one source. Just like it would be good to get three quotes for a building job, you should try and get three pieces of advice and then research the advice. Look at a scenario that is like yours, and at someone who has made success from a scenario like yours.

Some of the things I have written in this book, people will read and think that it is obvious, but saying that is obvious to some people, is like saying why don't they use their common sense? What is common to one person may not be common to the next.

Once we can understand that there are different angles, and different elements in conversation and advice, we can then piece it together like a jigsaw puzzle; and at the end, when we put all the pieces together, we can see the full picture. Once we understand the concept, then we can go around picking the right pieces, to fit into the right places, to get the right picture.

Chapter 22
Mission Statement

A *mission statement*[1] is defined as a business plan in summary.

In other words, take out the all singing and dancing business plan, strip it down to its bare bones, and there you have it, a straight forward mission statement.

To direct you through the maze of self-employment, you need a mission statement. Your mission statement can be made up of bullet points, using your own terminology; points that make sense to you.

An example of 'mission accomplished' was 'passing my driving test'. I was one of those young people who could not wait to pass my driving test! And fortunately, my father would allow me to drive his van on private land where a funfair was located from time to time.

The area was a bit like a dirt track, back in those days, when my father taught me to drive there. I was young,

---

[1] Definition:
'A formal summary of the aims and values of a company, organisation, or individual.'

around 16 and my father would give me regular lessons when he had days off work. As soon as I was 17, I put in for my driving test. Once I was notified of the date of my driving test, which was six weeks after my 17th birthday, I booked three lessons with a driving school, one each day for the three days leading up to my test. My third lesson was just before my test and I used the same vehicle to take my test. I took my driving test and I passed it first time. I was euphoric, now I was free! I saw myself as free as a bird.

The above example regarding my driving test is a positive example of an achievement. I am now going to show you the flipside, where your efforts, energy, and devotion to a cause, through no fault of your own, can bring you to a different outcome.

I have been to conferences where bank managers, and business advisors have made presentations, and have stated that if you want to start your own business, come to the bank. In fact, one of the banks used the strapline 'we are the listening bank'.

Here is an example of my mission impossible, my experience. I put together the most structured, definitive business plan, put on my best suit, minded my p's and q's and made an appointment with a high street Bank Manager. I looked at this as the most important business meeting I could have, with the most important document, I had ever had the pleasure to call my own. I prepared and rehearsed as I had never done before. I got to my appointment early, so that I was relaxed and ready to execute my most important business role.

I shook the Business Banking Manager's hand firmly, took a seat and smiled whilst I handed him the business plan. I followed his eyes, whilst he scrolled through each page, smiling back at me and nodding. I watched as he carefully closed the document and put it on his executive desk. Then he asked me a few questions about my background, and why I decided to go into business. There was a pause whilst the Business Banking Manager thinks, and then pops the big question, 'how much money would you like to borrow from our small business loan fund?' You think quickly and think to yourself, 'I'd better play it safe and ask for a small amount'.

Then there is a further silence, a smile, and then the pre-prepared very friendly 'no, we will need to see some activity on your account first, please try again in six months to a year's time. We pride ourselves on lending to new start-up businesses.'

In my experience, banks want to lend you money when they see you are doing well, so what we must do is create a scenario where the average person can start a business, using the minimal amount of money one can, and grow slowly. But be sure to cross all the 't's, dot all the 'i's, and gain momentum as you go along. This book is not about advising you on what to do, however it can give you an insight into my own personal business experiences, and examples of some of the pitfalls.

I have heard on several occasions, business advisers say, that if you want to start a business, borrow money from your family or friends, and I am thinking, 'are they for real?'

The number of stories you hear, of families and friends being torn apart, because one had lent another money, and the other was unable to pay it back. If you are all multi-millionaires, and you want to lend each other thousands of pounds, it is quite different. However, for the average person starting their own business, or trying to be self-employed, and bring home an average wage; they do not really have access to those family and friends, that will say 'here's a few thousand pounds, go and start your own business. It doesn't matter if it works out or not'.

People can be put off when they first start talking about going into business on their own. Especially if someone says to them, you need money to start a business. However, many people that are going to start their business on their own, is because they do not have money, and want to start a business to earn an income.

Some people start a business because they find it difficult getting a job, and some might not want to work for other people anymore, so it is about finding ways around this maze of self-employment. There are organisations, and government grants to help. If your business setup is dependent upon those structures that give grants, and you make grant applications that are unsuccessful, you may have to rethink your business strategy, and find one that is not dependent upon grants.

One of the ways to get started, is to think and plan how you will get customers. The fact that we are now in the age of the internet, there are many more ways you can get information about your business out there, and get people to know who you are, and what you do, so they can buy your product or service.

Chapter 23
Minority Mentality

The trouble with some minority businesses is that they target minority groups, they set up in minority areas, sell minority goods and only sell to minority clients. My concern with that, is that approximately 90% of the UK population is the majority, and only 10% of the population is the minority (in this case I am using the example of ethnic minority communities in the UK). You must see that from the beginning, you will have an uphill struggle.

One would think in business, that the bigger the pool you target, the more likely it is that your business will succeed. Therefore, the smaller the pool you target, the less likely it is that your business will be a success. Most of the major corporations target the majority, knowing that they will sweep up some of the minority within that group, which will eventually help their business become a success. If you turn it the other way around, the fact that you may sweep up some of the majority groups while targeting the minority, will be a very much smaller sum.

So, let us ask, why is it that some minority groups only target minority clients? I think some of it is about confidence. Many people, may feel a lot more confident, setting up businesses, in areas they are from, and with clients who will understand their products and services; and will come and support them, by buying their products or services.

In the age of the internet, companies of different sizes can have a similar presence online. The customer will not necessarily know, or care, how big or small you are, when they decide to buy your product or service.

It is important to, rather than just dip your toe in the water when you are going into business, to take a leap, and jump right in. If you have done the preparation, and market research, and tested the market, you will have a good idea what your customer wants to buy, and your business will most likely make a profit. The moral of my story is to think about the majority, not the minority, because it is better to have 10% of a huge market than 90% of a tiny market; it is down to you.

After several years of running my own businesses, I became a business link champion, through an organisation called Business Link. Business Link was a government-funded business advice and guidance service in England. It consisted of an online portal, managed by HM Revenue and Customs (HMRC) and a national telephone helpline.

As a business link champion, I became the Vice Chair of the Slough Leadership Challenge. This was a group of businesses that were brought together to talk about their businesses, to get business support, and to give business support to other business owners.

As Slough is an area that has a high population of Black, Asian, and Minority Ethnic (BAME) people, Business Link had business advisors trained to support and give advice to minority ethnic businesses. There was also the Knowledge Centre in London, an aspect of Business Links function, and this centre had a lot of knowledge about black and minority ethnic businesses. Although I believe that minority businesses should target not just minority, but also majority groups, there are certain aspects of business that are more pertinent to the minority ethnic community, than the majority businesses, and I think there is quite a lot of research out there, that will show this. Business Link based a lot of what they did, around relevant research.

Some people do not understand why minority ethnic support organisations exist, because they say that every-one should be treated the same. So, they may see these advisors that are supporting minority businesses, as showing favouritism.

However, in my experience, when a minority group is supported, it is supported in order to bring it up to a level where they are competing on par with the majority. So, it is not to make them any better or give them any extra support, but it is to give them support so that when they are competing against majority businesses, they have been brought up to a level where the competition is not so skewed against them.

Not everything in this book will make sense to you, because the concept of majority and minority may be new to you. The British culture includes cultures from overseas. Take one example: a group of English men meet at a pub after work on a Friday evening, they drink beer (English culture), and then they may go for an Indian meal or a Turkish kebab. These are now very much a part of the British culture too. So, as you can see sometimes different cultures mix and that is all good once we celebrate it positively. People tend to have fixed views on this, but sometimes the facts can help to explain the reality.

The Business Link organisation changed, and they then became on online portal. These support agencies or quangos, last just as long as the government, or as long as the politicians want them to last. When the money runs out, the organisation either disappears completely, or changes its name to attract a new tranche of funding.

There has been much information in the news about the underrepresentation of women as Chief Executives of major corporations. Some people argue that if women had the skills, and applied for these jobs, they would get them. Others say that it is the 'old boys network' where men, usually middle aged or older, look after each other, by only promoting people that look like themselves.

There are some very competent women Chief Executives of major corporations, albeit in the minority, who have got these jobs through their own blood, sweat and tears, only to find people telling them that they only got the job because they are a woman, in order to balance out the quotas.

Self-employment has an answer to this, because in my experience if you have what people want, and you do your due diligence, people will buy your service, and there are many products and services out in the market place, that people will buy irrespective of your gender or race. If you pitch your product or service right, your customers will come and purchase from you. In my experience, self-employment irons out the creases, and places us all on a level playing field.

Chapter 24
Business Location

I spent some time working with a small independent mobile phone retailer. I then bought into a small independent mobile phone shop in Henley-on-Thames. It was quite interesting as I did not know Henley-on-Thames, and I now had two employees to manage. The shop was on one of the high streets of this lovely town. What I did not know much about, was the culture of the town.

Once, I parked my care outside the shop to collect some phones in order to take them and have them reconnected. In those days people would reconnect second-hand phones and sell them on, and the Reading branch of the company did the reconnections. I was in the shop packing up the phones to take to Reading when a traffic warden came in and said, 'excuse me, is that your car?' I said 'yes, it is', and she said, 'well move it' and I thought hmm. 'You could see it's on double yellow lines, so move it' she said. I thought ok, I do not want to give the wrong impression in a new town that I am going be working in for a while. So, I put the first batch of boxes in the back of my car, and then I realised I had been given a parking ticket.

The Traffic Warden was not that far away so I said, 'excuse me you've just asked me to move my car, I've come straight out, and I have a parking ticket?' She said, 'yes I asked you to move it, I didn't say I wouldn't ticket it. If it were not on double yellow lines, I wouldn't have ticketed it, or asked you to move it.'

At this point, I thought she was being very unreasonable, but I carried on doing what I was doing. I put another batch of boxes in my car and went back into the shop. She followed me and said, 'I asked you to move the car, you haven't moved it, move it before I call the police', so I said, 'well I already have a ticket, I've got nothing to lose, so if you want to call the police, then call them.'

As I was putting the boxes in the car, a police car pulled up. The traffic warden had a conversation with the police officer, and then he came over to me and said, 'you were asked to move the car, why didn't you move it?'. I said, 'well officer, I didn't move the car because I wasn't given a chance to move it before I got a ticket, in fact she asked me to move it after she ticketed it, and I felt that was unreasonable'. He said, 'well where are you from?' I said, 'I'm from Reading, I've been working there for a while and learning the ropes, and I've come down here as this is part of a franchise'. He said, 'well this is Henley, not Reading, you better move the car now, or you might be liable to be arrested!!'. So, with that I took the last couple of boxes of phones, put them in the boot of the car, and proceeded to drive back to Reading, to get the phones reprogrammed to be reconnected.

There are certain things about business, the culture of a town, and the people you may work with, that you would not normally take into consideration in a business start-up, I certainly did not.

After that incident, I did not park outside the front on the double yellow lines. I found a place, slightly away from the shop, and I would walk with the boxes of phones to the shop from my car. It was a real eye opener, in regard to how different places have different cultures. I was used to traffic wardens in Reading saying, 'by the way, in just a few minutes can you move your car, or I will ticket it', and I would normally move it soon after. Sometimes, it is different in different towns and you will have to take that into consideration, that as a new person you may need to learn the culture of the town, as it may not be the same, as the place that you have come from.

The shop did quite well. However, at the time the mobile phone industry was changing, and the way the changes worked, meant that the second-hand phone market and the way the business worked, would change significantly. Normally, we would buy a mobile phone and get it connected, and as a supplier we would get commission for connecting that phone. If a person were unable to pay their bill, their phone would be disconnected, so they would sometimes end up selling the phone to businesses like ours. We could then reprogram that phone and reconnect it with somebody else. It would be like a brand-new phone with no bill, no history, all above board.

The second-hand phone market was buoyant. I think for security reasons, and many other reasons the mobile phone industry realised that peoples' phones were being stolen, and then reconnected, so something had to be done. The whole industry changed, and we could not reprogram a mobile phone in the same way as before. Basically, when you would buy a stock of phones, each phone would be brand new with warranty and instructions and we would then get the phone connected and sell it with a small profit.

I felt it was time to move on before all the major changes happened, so I managed to sell the shop, and move on to other things.

START
OWN BUSINESS
 Now
 Later
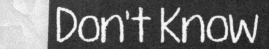 Don't Know

Chapter 25
Starting Up

When you begin your self-employed journey, you should be aware of where you stand legally, as you would not like to be prosecuted for trading illegally. Make an appointment with a business advisor, either independent, or connected to a government department. The job centre should be able to point you in the right direction.

To keep things simple and straight forward you can set yourself up as a 'sole trader', which means you trade under your own name.

You should not need a business advisor if you are just setting up as a sole trader. You will need an address, telephone number, bank account, and business stationery with your business name and contact details on. To open a bank account, you will need to take your proof of address, name, and photo ID; any utility bills should be dated within the last three months.

Be aware if you have had a County Court Judgment (CCJ) in the past, a mobile phone contract, or any other regular payment, that you have had difficulty in paying and have fallen behind on. Or if you have been taken to court for non-payments, or debts, you may find it diffi-cult to open a bank account. However, all is not lost. Search around and you may find a bank that is willing to open an account for you. You may also want to speak to an accountant, and a business solicitor before setting off on your journey.

Some businesses require a licence before they can start trading. I would advise that you research this, as diffe-rent businesses may require specific licences.

Starting a limited company by shares, is a different ball game altogether, as it is a different legal structure. I would suggest you get further information from a source that specialises in limited company set ups. It can be straight forward to set up a company, and there are companies that offer ready-made company names with governing document templates.

However, going back to dealing with self-employment as a sole trader. Be clear with your invoicing and pay-ment systems, also be sure to offer different ways of paying i.e. by cash, cheque, bank transfer, or even credit or debit card, using a card machine, or online.

Your intention should be to provide the best possible service, however a good way to validate your work, is to ask your customers for a review of the product or service you have provided. If they are happy to do this, you can then add it to your website, as people like to know how good your product/services are, from previous clients.

The UK offers you the opportunity to set up a business for next to nothing, so make sure you do your research on the business that you want to set up, as there is nothing like paying for information, advice, and guidance when you do not need to.

Remember the moto: Keep It Simple and Straightforward (KISS). The more straightforward it is, the easier it is to progress, and grow your business. Keep searching for knowledge. The more you know the more it shows.

Let's imagine, you have decided that you want to become a mobile hairdresser. You have been working in a hair salon for some time, whilst also doing some private work in your spare time. You have compared what the hair salon charges, to what you get paid for the same hairstyle privately, and you work out that becoming a mobile hairdresser, without the overheads of a premises with rent, rates, lighting, and heating, could provide the same service for less money, to your customers. Although it is not a good idea to steal customers from your employer, when you decide to move on there is nothing wrong with letting your customers know that you are going it alone, and they can contact you on your mobile telephone for updates. That way it is then up to the customer to decide which way they want to go.

As a self-employed mobile hairdresser, you would need various industry insurances to cover you against legal costs, and compensation payments, resulting from any injuries to a client, attributed to you as a result of any successful claim against you.

You will also need equipment, such as a hairdryer, brushes, clippers, scissors, tongs, towels, and a tunic etc.

If you are visiting clients at their own home, you may need a vehicle to transport you and your equipment, which means you would need a driving licence, insurance to cover you as a self-employed person driving to and from client's homes, a vehicle excise licence, and a valid MOT certificate, if your vehicle is more than three years old. It may seem a lot, but it is a legal requirement to keep you and your clients safe. In terms of health and safety, you might also want to prepare some risk assessments, to ensure that you have investigated your business that might have some element of risk attached to it, and then try to eliminate that risk by adding safety measures.

Keeping up to date with changes in government legislation, that may affect your business, is also important. Regular trade magazine subscriptions can provide additional specialist information. It is up to you to be compliant; ignorance is no excuse.

Some of the more obvious things are essential, like keeping a diary to make sure you do not double book. Your timekeeping must be impeccable, your hygiene must be on point, and you must demonstrate the highest level of integrity.

If you are going to be late because of something that could not be helped, phone your client, giving them as much notice as possible, in case they need to rebook. Ensure that clients can get hold of you by phone, text, email, through the internet, and by social media, and be flexible with appointments, by making them around your customers as much as you can.

The most important role when working for yourself, is to never underestimate making time for your mental and physical health. There are so many books, and hundreds of pages on the internet dedicated to this subject, you will not be in short supply of how to look after yourself with the do's and don'ts. You can decide whether to follow one piece of advice, or more. You can mix and match the information, just be sure to take your trade seriously and look after yourself.

Chapter 26
Marketing/Communication

Far too often, sole traders see marketing as unimportant, and something that only large companies and corporations with big marketing budgets, and departments do.

I have a slightly different view on marketing[2].

It is my assertion that all of us, in some shape or form is marketing, sometimes consciously, and at other times unconsciously.

You see it is not always about big marketing campaigns, where you have big posters, or even small leaflets that you drop through people's letter boxes, or flyers that are put in newspapers. That does not have to be the way marketing is done, it can be done, by word of mouth, and through your smart phone in terms of texts, WhatsApp, and other social media applications. Marketing can also be done through email marketing, and mailouts.

---

[2] The oxford dictionary definition of marketing is: *'The action or business of promoting and selling products or services, including market research and advertising.'*

There are many ways that marketing can be done, to let people know about your product or service, and I think it is sometimes overlooked far too much, by sole traders.

My view is that you can do it in some of the ways mentioned above, which can be quite cost effective. In large marketing companies, they really do spend major money, and it does not always reap the rewards or responses, that they may be looking for.

One of the ways you could get free or reduced rate marketing, is by getting an advertorial done in a magazine or newspaper. You will get interviewed, and the interviewer will speak to you about what you do, and your experiences of how you are getting on. Most of the time, this type of feature is free of charge.

There is also local radio; they are always looking for local people to talk about what they are doing, and what type of products or services they have to offer. There are these ways and more, such as using YouTube, as a way of connecting with a larger audience.

There are many ways to market, and it does not really matter what you do, in terms of what your trade or business is. There are people who say, 'my business doesn't need marketing', or 'marketing doesn't work for what I do', but it does.

It is important to manage the marketing of your product or service, and to ensure that it is targeted to the right people, and in the right way.

I believe that marketing should not be underestimated. It is a particularly important feature that must be a part of you, and your business.

Let us take a trip down memory lane, in order to simplify the notion of how we market, even unconsciously.

In the 1980s, on most weekends I used to go to the disco, and youth clubs, with friends. We were a group of well-dressed lads enjoying ourselves, all single, and wanting to grow up as fast as we could. In the back of our minds, we would be thinking of always making a good impression, so the way we dressed, danced, and spoke, was with this in mind. We wanted to be popular, so we promoted ourselves in every way, without any training or experience. A few years later in business whilst looking for clients, I realised I already have what it takes to win business.

Back when I first became self-employed, there was no social media, imagine you become a second-hand car dealer, and you pick up an unbelievably cheap car that needs some work done. You have some contacts in the motorcar industry, some old friends that can get you parts cheap, and help you out until you sell the car for a profit, pay them what you owe, and pocket the difference. You could pick a motor trader magazine and read some advertisements that are similar to the car that you are selling and take some really good photos with your mobile phone, in a well-lit area. Armed with your description and your top-quality photos, you post an advertisement on a popular advertising website, and for a few pounds you have done some marketing and advertising.

The beauty of this is that you now have your car online with access to many buyers. To the discerning buyer your advertisement is as professional as anyone else trying to sell their car, so do not be put off by the fact that you may not have as much money as your competitors. It is all about presentation, the way you market and promote your goods or service. Push yourself, you will be surprised at what you can achieve if you believe. My late father used to quote 'The race is not for the swift, or the battle for the strong, but for those who can endure'.

In life we interact with different people that come from different backgrounds. Also, some people from within the same community, can have different social backgrounds, and some people from different backgrounds, can be part of the same social groups.

I think a part of our social skills, is to be able to interact with different people in our community. Communication is a powerful tool. We need to communicate to customers, and suppliers, whether we are self-employed, or run a business.

If the communication breaks down, it is highly likely that you would be left with an unhappy customer. We must also take note of our body language when we are communicating. The way you stand, look, listen, and move are all especially important.

You may go to someone's house, because you are doing some work there, but even something as simple as taking your shoes off, providing there are no health and safety requirements, could show how you understand people, their customs, and traditions.

A customer might not fully know what it is they want you to do, so you must ensure that you can practice active listening, they can then see that you are not just listening to answer quickly, but listening, and taking in what they are saying. You can respond in a way that shows you are generally concerned with what they want.

Sometimes, you must be positive, you know what you offer your customers, and you need to be positive, and confident enough, to explain to them in a way that they understand. You want them to be a happy customer. The way you talk, and how you talk (not shout, not talk too fast, not talk too quietly), is important when you are self-employed, and trying to speak to people about what you do, and how you do it.

As great a job as you might be doing, you may have a situation where a customer is not fully satisfied. You show empathy, by showing them that you understand that they are not satisfied. Remember the customer is always right. Be sincere and explain to them what the scenario is, but remember when you leave that customer, you are leaving that customer not only happy, regarding what you have done for them, but you are leaving the customer in a way that they feel better about themselves. Then they would be happy to recommend you to others.

Word of mouth is one of the most powerful ways of getting continuous business recommendations, so ensure you remember that in your own self-employment.

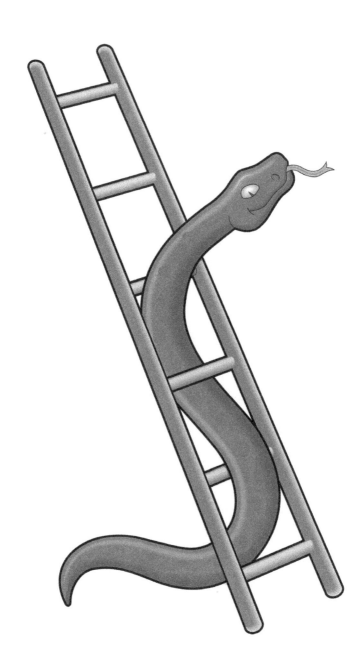

Chapter 27
Snakes and Ladders

When I was in my twenties, I remember my father would say to me 'Keith, why don't you hang your hat where you can reach it?', and I would reply to my father, 'Dad, I can always get a ladder to reach my hat'. The analogy was that I would speak to my father about my business ideas, and even though he believed in me, I think he felt I was thinking too big, too quickly.

My father, like many concerned parents, would advise me to slow down, or play it safe. I knew that was sensible advice, however the advice did not fit with my vision. There was something in my veins, driving me to keep reaching, keep thinking that I can continue going, however outlandish it might have sounded at the time.

That is why I have called this chapter *Snakes and Ladders*, because that was, and still is my approach. My father's analogy of hang your hat where you can reach it, actually meant 'Keith, just play it safe with what you're going to do, and any business you're going into'. However, there is no fun, danger, or excitement in playing it safe. I like to push the boundaries. Rather than hanging my hat where I can reach it, I hang it higher than I can reach it, and somehow, I climb a ladder to get there.

In the popular board game called 'Snakes and Ladders', you throw some dice, and with the number they land on and add up to, you move a counter along numbered squares on the board, that also contains pictures of snakes and ladders. If the number on the dice you throw takes you to a number that makes you land on a snake, you slide your counter down the snake to a lower number. If you get a number that makes you land on a ladder, you take your counter up the ladder, closer to the end of the game. The aim of the game is to win by reaching the highest number on the board first.

In a way, I do not think business is that dissimilar to the game of Snakes and Ladders. Throwing dice is a game of chance. When we go into business, unlike throwing a dice and waiting for what number we receive, we are hoping that we can use our judgement to see where we can land on the board. If you look at life as a board game and continue to throw dice with numbers that will get you up the ladders, the further you go up the board, the more successful you are.

However skilled, experienced, and qualified you are, you are guaranteed that there are going to be some people that are like snakes, who will try and bring you down. Sometimes, you will find some people like ladders that can take you years ahead of where you would normally be, or you could again land on a square with a snake and be back to where you may have been two, or even three years ago. That is the game of Snakes and Ladders. That is the game of business.

Another question is, how can we put ourselves in a position, where we land on more ladders, than snakes? I suppose this is where experience comes into play. This is where the information that we have at our fingertips, and our perseverance, comes into play. If we can ensure that we keep going, until we land on enough ladders on our journey, and that we are eradicating the snakes, then that is definitely an avenue for success.

Instead of seeing the snakes, and ladders, as threats, and opportunities, the snakes, and ladders, can be seen as people. These can be the people that you surround yourself with, or people that surround, or hang around you. We can have people around us that are only there to benefit themselves, so they are like the snakes, they take, take, take. For these people, you are their ladder, but they become your snake. What you do not realise is that they are zapping you, of your energy, they are zapping you, of your information. They are there to see what tips they can pick up from you.

Some people, maybe because of their lack of confidence, or the circumstances of where they live, surround themselves with lots of snakes. That is not good in business. It is more purposeful to surround yourself with many ladders. People who are ladders are influential people, more knowledgeable, experienced, and have different skills to you, and they can be your ladders.

The information that you share with these types of people, moves you up the ladder, and the information that they share with their colleagues about you, moves you up the ladder too. They signpost you to people that will also move you up the ladder. They are committed to your success, and they want to bring you along with them. These are rare people.

Sometimes, people find it more difficult to hang around, and surround themselves with people who are brighter than them, because they feel somewhat lacking. But all the experiences, that other people have acquired, are experiences that you can draw from, and use to move yourself further on in business.

If you look around your circle of acquaintances, even as you read this book, you should be able to identify the snakes, the people that bring you down, and the ladders, the people that lift you up. It may not be advisable to tell the snakes, that you view them as snakes, because they may get offended, but I am sure people that you view as ladders would be happy to be viewed in that way.

We use different words for ladders in business terms, like mentors, advisors, or business colleagues, and they are the people you can connect to, to achieve in business. We must be able to find these people, who will have positive influences on us. We must be able to spend time with them, and we must be able to share information with them, because if you have a ladder in your life, you can also be a ladder to them. Although some people may be ahead of you in some aspects of business, you may be ahead of them in other aspects of life, and that synergy could work wonders.

Chapter 28
Pricing

Pricing - one of those things that some people find quite difficult. How do you know how much you are worth? How do you know how much someone would pay for your product or service?

We know if you under-price yourself, your customers might think you are delivering a substandard product or service. However, if you price yourself too high, people might think you are ripping them off, but it is not as straight forward as that, because how do you know how to value something?

You can go to a supermarket, and buy a branded box of cereal, even though the supermarkets' own brand, is cheaper. You then open it, only to discover it looks the same as the supermarket version. If the supermarkets own brand is less expensive, does it mean it is bad for you? Or the one that is more expensive, is better for you? These might be the kind of questions, that go around in people's head, when they are thinking of setting up their own business, and trying to do a comparison price list. I do not have the answer to this question. I think it is like, 'how long is a piece of string?'

Many of us in the past, may have sold a car, and what we tend to do, is look online at the most popular car selling websites. We find a car that is the same year as the one we are selling, with a similar mileage. It has the same number of doors and the same equipment, whether it has electric windows, automatic or manual transmission, a CD player, or satnav system. We match it to a few vehicles, and then price it around those prices. However, it is quite different if you are selling a product or service that is rare. Maybe you can compare it with something that is equivalent, and use that as a benchmark, to price up your product or service.

It is quite interesting, the way that the human brain works. If you undercut someone in terms of their price, and it is a substantial amount, that could ring alarm bells for potential customers, who may think, 'no I'm not going there.' The pricing itself is what is putting them off. If you really believe in what you are doing, you should be able to charge a premium price for it, and people will pay extra, for something that offers extra, or is better.

Consumers will pay more for something that is rare, and if that describes your product or service, then you can price it for more than your competitors. Of course, it must be good, because if it is not, you will get found out fast and word will spread, which could put you out of business. It really does depend on what you do, how you do it, and who you compare yourself to.

If you are a painter and decorator, you can look in the newspaper to see the prices that painters and decorators charge per day. You can also telephone some of them as a customer, and they will give you a quote, so you will have an idea of how much they charge. You can use this knowledge to help you decide how much you should charge. Although it is not just about knowing how much they charge, you need to know how long it would take them. To find out what people will pay, you will have to obtain a lot of information, to get a fair price for your product or service.

We do have the tendency, (especially people that are new to business and are nervous about taking money from people), to under-cut our competitors, rather than go in at a competitive price, and that is not good. It is important to back up your price with some good reviews. Make sure you have reviews, and if you have a website, encourage your customers to leave comments about how good your products/services are.

It is particularly important to ensure that those comments are true, and that you are not fabricating a false history for your services. I am talking about genuine comments on your website, that says doing business with you, including the customer service, price, and after-sales were excellent or at least good.

Whether you are painting someone's house, or selling someone a product, guarantee the product and the work, so that if they have a problem they can come back to you, and you will replace or repair it. You do this because this could work well for you going forward, as people will recommend you to their family and friends. This will give your business a boost.

So, my tips are:

- compare your pricing with your competitors
- do an excellent job and provide an aftersales service

To create a scenario where you can have longevity, you would need to capitalise on other aspects of your skills. Whether it is a product or service, you will eventually need to diversify, which can mean different things to different people.

What is diversification? It is doing what you do, and how you do it, but differently. For example, somebody calls you to paint some rooms in their house, because you are a painter and decorator. You have always relied on your painting skills because that is the skill you mainly promote. You then find that you can add an extra element to your service, by asking your customer 'would you like some wallpaper put up?', and the customer might say, 'I was looking for someone that can wallpaper'. Then you get the job, you are happy, and the customer is happy. That is just one example of diversifying.

Diversifying can be done in many ways, you could be a barber, and you have a barber shop, and you spend most of your time cutting hair, and renting out chairs to other barbers. One day a customer comes in with his sister, and says his sister wants her hair braided, or some hair extensions. This would be the perfect reason to look for someone who can braid hair and put in hair extensions. You then rent a chair to that person, and you have different customers visiting your barbershop.

I have my own experience of diversifying. In the past, doing financial advising, mainly dealing with mortgages, insurance, and life insurance, I expanded the business by brokering finance for motor vehicles. So, diversifying can work in many ways.

A lady I know, who used to do typing, would hire out her services and type documents for people. She was also involved in community groups and was trained by those groups to produce annual reports and newsletters. Eventually she was able to add annual reports and newsletters to the services she offered.

In business, we must ensure that we are not a one trick pony, look at what your customers and clients want. Look at the other services, or skills that you have, or how you can add to what you have, and make it your duty to diversify. The more you can learn, the more you can earn. Remember, a happy customer, is a repeat customer.

Another string to add to your bow, and an advantage to your business, is to replicate your services/products. There is no cap on how many different products or services you can offer a client. In marketing, it is said that selling to a current or previous customer, is so much easier than selling to a new customer.

As a supplier of goods or services, make yourself 'head and shoulders' above the rest. It can be reflected in your prices. Put them slightly higher than your competitors' if what you offer is better.

Always bear in mind, that customers can go out and find other people that are doing the same things that you are doing, so you must stand out from the rest. You must have the edge, no short cuts, no doing things on the cheap, or rushing, ending up with a poor standard. Build a customer base and use your talents and experiences, that you have obtained from other aspects of this university of life. More than anything else, make sure what you do counts.

Chapter 29
Getting Paid

One would have thought that anyone who is going to embark upon becoming self-employed, would cover themselves to ensure that they get paid. Unbelievably, some people are quite nervous to ask for their money when they have finished doing the work. In some ways, it is probably easier to give a product to someone, and ask for the money, than to deliver a service, and request the money.

Getting paid is something that forms part of your contract, you do some work, you get paid, or you hope it's that simple. However, people will often dispute what they thought they were paying, when the job started, and when they expected to pay.

There are so many disagreements around this aspect, and you should really cover both parties with legal documentation, that has been agreed, signed, and dated by both sides, with a witness signature.

There is also another angle to consider. What if the customer says they are not happy with the work that has been done? How does that affect the payment? Will they pay and dispute it, or will they withhold the payment, and ask you to fix the problem that they are not happy with first? There is some form of arbitration, people can go to, where independent people can listen to both sides, and then decide.

Taking someone to court for not paying, can be an expensive course of action, especially if you employ a solicitor. Sometimes, it can be more expensive when you do not. So, what you do, and however you do it, it would be wise to employ a solicitor and have agreements in place.

Another thing that tends to happen, is when people thought they had a verbal agreement in place about a service, and when it is time for you to get paid, it seems one side has a selective memory, or there was some miscommunication between the parties.

Sometimes people can ask for work to be done, yet they only have a certain budget, and you have continued the work beyond that limit, and they are now unable to pay.

There can be so many different reasons why, at the end of the job, the deal, or the contract, there is some confusion about payment. Let us not take this aspect lightly, it can cause people to fall out, fight, and can result in people going to court.

It is important to ensure that any licences your business needs are all in date, so you can continue with your work. It is equally important to make sure that you do not assume the payment is going to be straight forward, because you may be in for a surprise.

Just to recap, getting paid is something that you must sort out before you commence the work, and let's face it, getting paid is what it's all about!

There are many modes of payment, and here is my take on some of the different methods.

Cheque

Banks seem to be trying to phase out cheques as they become outdated. I totally agree because the customer must write out the cheque, sign, and date it, and then you must bank the cheque, and after all that, you then must wait at least three working days for the money to clear in your account, before you can access the funds.

Under some circumstances, you may be the unfortunate receiver of a cheque that is marked 'refer to drawer'. This would mean that for some reasons the bank is unable to honour the cheque, usually because there are insufficient funds in the bank account that the cheque was drawn from, and this means that you will not receive the money, even though you accepted the cheque in good faith.

Card

To be able to accept payment by credit or debit card is very straight forward. You will first be required to acquire a portal which includes a machine. The card is inserted into the machine, however payments up to a certain amount can now be paid contactless if the machine supports this technology. Once the card is inserted into the card reader, the vendor will type in the amount to be paid by the customer. The customer would then be requested to check the amount is correct and enter their unique four-digit PIN (personal identification number). Providing there is enough funds available in the customer's account, the payment is authorised, and the money will be transferred to your account, usually within a couple of days.

Electronic Transfer

Electronic transfer can be done online, via mobile banking, or over the telephone, via telephone banking. Some customers prefer to transfer payments directly to an account, and electronic payments are usually imme-diate payments. If you are an online banking customer with access to a computer and the internet, or a mobile telephone, you will be able to check if the funds have been received.

Online payments have been growing rapidly over recent years. There are now a few online payment companies that you can pay your money to via a credit or debit card, or through the bank, and these companies guarantee that they will transfer the money to the destination you have requested. These new ways of accepting payments on your behalf, are all quite straightforward to use. The disadvantage is that sometimes those companies will deduct their commission directly, before forwarding you your money.

Cash

As the saying goes 'Cash is King'. This saying seems to be less and less relevant as time goes on, however people still like to pay cash for certain products and services. One of the most obvious drawbacks is that you have to count the money to make sure it is correct, whilst also checking the notes to make sure that they are not counterfeit. And then take the cash to the bank where the cashiers also count and check it before they give you a receipt. It all seems very time consuming, so cash may have been 'King' back in the day, however, there seems to be more direct forms of payment nowadays.

Chapter 30
Don't Blame the Fridge

I would like you to step back and consider, that as an individual you may believe that the circumstances you are in, are not within your control, instead you have attributed this to someone else.

Just think about it, and then think about how many times you may have done that. Then think about the people around you and how many times they may have blamed you for things, and you have thought 'well that has nothing to do with me, that is your responsibility'.

The reason I say to think about this, is because many times, until we are put in a specific situation, and put in someone else's shoes, it is only then that we see things from a perspective other than our own. 'The grass is not always greener on the other side.'

I do not say this in a negative context, in fact I say it in a positive context, because it seems that when people are put in a situation that is new to them, and they truly have been able to experience something that they have never understood, and they have sat back and watched other people experience it, it is then that the realisation comes home.

We all get caught up in our own lives, wallow in our own sorrow, so much that we often cannot see the wood from the trees, but it is like driving with mud on your windscreen, then you activate the windscreen wipers, that subsequently wipe away the mud and you can see again and move forward. I hope this is a perspective we can all appreciate.

Don't you think it is astonishing that people can apportion blame to any circumstance that they may find themselves in. And in doing that, it seems to give them some justification for their predicament. Yes, this does include you, and yes it does include me. In some way, we are all hypocrites. However, recognising this perhaps is a step forward in redeeming ourselves of this condition. The condition I shall refer to as the blame culture, and that's why I'm saying, *'don't blame the fridge'*.

There are some people who are unemployed, they have been unemployed for some time, months, and some people even years. They have been unable to obtain gainful employment and they blame it all on everything else but themselves, this is akin to the person that continues to gain weight, and will not take responsibility for what they are eating, and then they blame the fridge, or what's in the fridge, or what's in the cupboard, or 'buy one get one free', not going to the gym enough, slow metabolism, getting older, work, anything but themselves.

What I am saying is simply, don't blame the fridge. I can also say, don't blame the person who interviewed you for you not getting the job, don't blame the traffic warden for giving you a parking ticket, when you parked your car on double yellow lines, don't blame the bar person who served you the drink for you getting drunk, I could go on and on, about where people place the blame. Because we seem to be living in this blame culture and if you find someone or something else to blame; if you are not taking responsibility, then how can you fix the problem?

Just a shift of thinking to 'I'm responsible for this', I'm no longer going to spend too much time and energy on that, that I can't control, and I'm going to start spending my time and energy on that, that I can.

There is a big difference between taking care of what is here, what's now and what's around you, then complaining about what's over there, and not directly around you. You see some people believe that good luck is why people do well, and bad luck is why people do not. People like me believe that you can make luck, rather than wait for good or bad luck to make you, or your circumstances change.

Although I agree that there are some things that happen to us that are out of our control, that are a force of nature that we could not avoid, because we were in the wrong place at the wrong time. But that is not the things we are referring to here. We are talking about lifting theirs, and other people's spirits. Showing people that they can do it. Believing in people when they do not even believe in themselves. We should consistently remind people 'don't blame the fridge'.

How many people have you met, that you know want to give up smoking? But when you speak to them, they tell you what they are doing about giving up smoking. You then question whether you believe they really do, or whether they believe they really do want to give up smoking.

How many people want to give up eating cake or junk food, and then when you ask them what they are doing about it, you will then question, do they really want to give up, or are they just saying they want to give up, because they think that is the right thing to say.

How many people have you been with, and they say 'oh, I just don't like that person there, or I hate this person', and when you question them about the person, they say, its someone they have never even met, its someone they may or may not have seen on television, or someone they may have heard something about through the grapevine. But those negative thoughts supersede the positive thoughts, rather than saying, I don't have an opinion on that person because I don't really know them, other than what people say, it seems that many people are far too ready to put people down, or to dislike people, sometimes to even despise people that they don't know.

We need to take control of our emotions, actions, feelings, approach, view, what we say and what we do. Let us lend a helping hand to people who are less fortunate, or people who have fallen on hard times, people who are ill or disabled, people who are too proud to say they need help, and let us do it without gloating about it, without telling the whole world that we helped that person, as if were waiting for an award.

To feel good about ourselves, we must help people feel good about themselves. Sometimes, we must just do it out of the goodness of our hearts, and smile to ourselves when we see somebody else succeed, and feel positive about people that have achieved, and those good vibes we wish for everybody else, will come back to us in abundance.

Celebrate everyone, take responsibility, stand strong, and help others.

Chapter 31
Continued Learning

Just when I thought I knew it all, I started meeting more people who knew much more than I did, and this really bothered me. Some of the people knew a little more than me, and some of the people knew so much more than me. I continued to bump into people like this at different meetings and various events that I attended, so it was to my horror that I felt, in terms of my knowledge, I was going backwards fast. This was not good enough.

It was the first time in my life that I had started to have negative thoughts about my achievements. I started thinking that maybe I only surrounded myself with people that have less knowledge than me to look and feel better. I started to question my confidence and whether it was real, or whether I had a lack of confidence and I was masking it with perceived confidence, so that other people believed that I knew more than I did, or that I felt better than I did.

I was in a conundrum, what do I do? How do I deal with this? Up until this point it was quite easy for me to manoeuvre my way through things, around things, under things, over things, but here I was in my mid 30's and I was stuck. I felt almost as if a fuse had blown in my head. But after some thinking time, and looking at the different opportunities available to me, I decided to enrol on a course.

It had to be quite a high-level course, and I had to believe that it was something I could achieve. I enrolled myself onto a course that was delivered by Buckinghamshire University. It was for a post graduate qualification in business management. Now this was a challenge and I thought "I'm up for this". However, at the beginning it was an uphill struggle, it was hard. I had not been in education for years, and there were words and terminology that I did not understand, and I was not as up to speed with using computers as some of the other students.

Nevertheless, I persevered and after two years I succeeded. I felt good about my achievement, and I had proven that to myself, and I now have a piece of paper to prove myself to others. Even though I had attained a post-graduate qualification, that was not enough. I felt an itch and thought 'I'm going to take this a step further and do something different'.

I then enrolled on a Thames Valley University course to complete a post graduate qualification in further education teaching. Again, this was a very challenging course, and we even had teachers there that were updating their training. We had to complete individual learning plans, which some of the former teachers on the course had not done before, so although they were already in teaching, they were learning new things on the course. Some of them were quite stubborn, because since they had been teaching for years, they thought that they did not need to change their way of teaching. Surprisingly though, bit by bit, they changed.

I was learning with people who had many years' experience in teaching, and also learning alongside people who were stubborn about the changes required, as they refreshed their knowledge. I liked many of the people I met on the course.

There were some challenging times, some funny times, and some serious times. We had to do micro teaching: standing up and presenting to the class. We learnt a bit more about each other and overall, it was extremely thorough. After coming away from that course, I felt I could focus on business. I now have two sets of post-graduate qualifications, that I can use to inform me going forward.

The icing on the cake for me in gaining the teaching qualification was that I then put together a course and called it 'An introduction to Self-employment'. I included the experiences I gained, over the many years of my own self-employment. I wrote the course using plain language, taking out unnecessary terminology, making it more straight forward for participants, showing them that they too can take the plunge into self-employment.

I have been in business for many years, even taking into consideration the times when I was in-between businesses. Throughout that time, I have also held various positions within many voluntary and charitable organisations.

The significance of these positions is the learning aspect of being involved in voluntary/charitable groups. Legislation within the voluntary and charity sector, changes just as regularly as it does in the private sector. When you meet as a committee you go through the usual day to day issues associated with your organisation and review any circulated paperwork from funders and statutory bodies (such as the Charity Commission, grant making organisations or local authorities), to keep informed of the best way to run the organisation. You can also learn skills from other committee members as some of them are in business themselves, and some of them might share with you their experiences.

In summary, *continued learning* can come from formal routes such as university, and training courses, or informal routes, such as sharing experiences with people, reading, and observations.

Reading is a great way to develop your understanding of business. The trouble is finding the time to read, whilst running a business. The way I have conquered this is to wait until I am travelling and flying long haul. I usually travel long haul at least once a year, and I purchase a business book to read whilst I am flying, relaxing on the beach in warmer climates, or to read wherever I am staying, whether at a hotel or with family.

The best books I have found, are autobiographies of successful people in business, sport, and other disciplines. These books give you an insight into the sacrifices that people have made to become successful, and the difficulties they have encountered.

Some of the books forewarn you of the pitfalls, and some emphasise the enjoyment of the journey. Overall, they are fantastic for informing you of the different terrains you may have to conquer on your way, and that perseverance usually pays off.

Chapter 32
Know what you don't know

It seems that throughout our schooling and development as young children, we have had all emphasis put on what we should know and learn, and in my opinion, not enough emphasis has been placed on what we don't know.

I think it's important that you should be mindful when entering a new business sector, or a brand-new business entity that you have not been in before, that you *'know what you don't know'*.

It may come as a surprise, or it may come as something that does not make any sense, but I am sure you are going to get the hang of what I am saying after reading this chapter. It is imperative that you know what you don't know, and there are good reasons for this.

I was introduced to a woman, by a friend of mine who I have known ever since I have been in business, and I was told that she was looking to give up the lease of her café. This café was in Reading town centre at a particularly good spot and there was parking outside. It was also on a main bus route in and out of the town centre.

The café was in good condition with pleasant décor. It had an outside area at the back, where people could sit and smoke, and overall, the price was affordable. However, I had never owned a cafeteria, but I thought since I had almost 25 years business experience at the time, and ate out a lot, then this should not be a major challenge.

I spoke with a friend of mine, who agreed that we would go and see the woman. We visited the café, and we decided to put our money together and take on the lease. We put out word to the community that we were looking for a chef, and that we were looking for staff. We decided to change the table covers and cutlery. We agreed the menu, put together a staff team, and started trading.

The woman that we took over the lease from, used to run her café early in the morning from about 7.00 am, and close after lunch. We decided to open the café around 12 noon and close about 11.00 pm at night. We got leaflets designed, and printed, wrote letters, used the internet to email, and sent text messages to all our friends, family, and community groups. We asked our friends, and family, to do the same. We then had a big launch with the local media in attendance.

It ran quite well at the beginning. We found new suppliers, and we also spoke to the local authority, and got to learn very quickly about how to run a café. After about a year, we decided to relinquish the lease to someone who had shown some interest, as we were unable to grow the café, and we were unable to capitalise on what we thought would be something very straightforward.

Some of the staff relationships were occasionally quite strained, and we basically decided that it was a very steep learning curve, but we must leave it to people who knew a bit more than we did. So, knowing what you don't know, can be very helpful in business. It can save you a lot of money, time, and heartache, because not knowing what you don't know, is worse.

Far too often, people are providing a service, and they look around not seeing the entirety of what happens, and think 'oh I can do that', but the term 'experience' is not something that people should take lightly, the term 'trading' is also not something someone should take lightly, or indeed the term 'qualified', because I believe if we had all of these three words together, we would perhaps be still be running the café today, and it may have been very successful.

I must admit, and I am telling you straight, that I underestimated what goes on behind the scenes in running a café, or in fact a business that incorporates cooked food on a day to day basis. I now have the utmost respect for chefs, café, restaurant, and takeaway owners, because it is not just the everyday planning, dealing with the food, dealing with staff, and keeping up to date with the current legislation.

The things I underestimated most were things like, the different temperatures that the fridge needs to be kept at, different coloured chopping boards for the different meats, vegetables, fish and so on. The fact that you would date foods that you would put in the fridge, so you know how long they can be kept before you must discard them. The fact that the hot food you serve must be a certain temperature when it is served. The cutlery, plates, and equipment need to be washed at a certain temperature, which includes the pots, and pans, etc.

I could go on, and I could write a whole book, on the misgivings regarding what it took to run a café. I take my hat off to those who work in the industry, I take my hat off to you. The staffing, the supervisions, the training and so on are very much like running other businesses, however because it involves food, there is an extra level of care that must be taken, to ensure that people do not leave your premises after consuming something and become ill.

The skills that chefs need, the fact that you need someone to come in at short notice if the chef is ill, and that person does not have the necessary skill set, to reproduce the food to the same quality as what your usual chef produces, so that your customers' experience is no different, can be a real challenge.

The constant cleaning throughout the day, not only of the kitchen, but the other areas of the establishment, like the WC and bathrooms, and main dining area, was also something we did not take into consideration at the beginning of the business.

One of the benefits of being self-employed is that I had flexibility. However, when you are running a business, and you are employing staff, you tend to get sucked back into working all hours. What I did not realise was that a catering business would get me into hours that I consider completely unsociable; it was an early morning start, to go and open up, and to collect fresh fruit and vegetables.

Sometimes, I was driving for two hours to pick up fresh produce, and then we were not finishing until between 12 midnight and 1.00 am, for up to six days a week. So, you can imagine my disappointment in opening a business, working all hours under the sun, it was like running from the frying pan into the fire.

Whatever business suits you, may not suit me; however, it is especially important to enjoy yourself whilst you master your craft. Be sure to work out what hours you are required, and whether you can dedicate that time to the business you decide to run.

Chapter 33
Managing people

In terms of recruitment, hiring people is something that always feels good to me. However, sometimes when the honeymoon period is over, and peoples' real personalities come through, they can be a nightmare to manage.

I dislike *managing people*. I am not sure that I am cut out for it, I am not sure I have that mean edge when it comes to firing people, that is not me.

I do not think it is something you can train to be, or you could just wake up in the morning and say, "ok I'm that person".

I am not from the old school, way of managing. I was managed by people who I would consider as old school types of managers. They were frightening, and I vowed, I would never be that type of person. That does not make it easier though, I think it makes it more difficult, because if you believe you are a people person, then you take on many aspects of managing people and their issues, which perhaps are not helpful to running a successful business.

I have managed all different types of people: male, female, young, not so young, Black, White, Asian, highly qualified, and not so highly qualified, some with a good command of English, some with less fluency, people with different cultures, loud, quiet, all sorts of people.

In the workplace, if somebody is not feeling well, they must take time off work to recover. Or maybe they are late, and then ask to speak to you in the office, so you have a one to one meeting. You are then expected to be a kind of counsellor, or social worker to deal with their issues; they may just need a shoulder to cry on.

Whether the staff member is a good or bad person, or if you are a good or bad manager, I think it is still going to be such a minefield. I have taken part in personal development training, as well as manager training. I have read books about personal development, business development and managing businesses, and yes you do get some tips, but it does not really help you when the reality sinks in, and someone comes to see you.

For example, if someone comes to see you and their child is sick, or someone in their family is sick, then they must take some time off. Many of these situations are covered with employment legislation in terms of how you should respond, or what you can and cannot allow, but we are all human, and with or without legislation we should be able to respond in an appropriate and caring manner. Does that mean I am a soft manager, who people think they can walk all over? Or does that mean that I am understanding when it comes to managing people? If that is the case, do people then take advantage of that? You see, it is not straightforward.

How do you dismiss someone knowing their situation, what would happen to them and their family? How can you tell someone 'no', by looking at their CV and seeing from their employment history, that they do not stay at workplaces for too long? Do you take them on anyway and hope that you can provide stability, or do you just take the strictly business view and say no? Based on their history, we may feel that they will do this again in the future, and we do not want to take that on.

All these questions are imperative when you are employing people. If you are working alone then you will not have these issues, but I have been in a situation employing 30 people. Some people might not think that is a lot, but that is thirty different personalities, and thirty different families. Thirty different reasons for having thirty different problems, thirty days in a row, what do I do?

As a human, I know that someone could be lying, but most of the time we just need to take on people based on face value and listen to what they have to say and act on it. I believe if you are a manager where staff are scared to approach you, and they are suffering in silence with a personal tragedy, then you are heading for a company that will not be successful overall.

If your employees genuinely believe you care about them, and their families, then you will get the best from them, and they will get the best from your employment.

People spend the most productive hours of their day at work, and usually by the time they return home, they are tired and not as sharp or alert as they had been at work. Anyone spending their most productive hours being miserable are not likely to be productive, but if the working environment is pleasant and people are focused, the workforce will not be looking forward to retiring early.

I have read stories about multimillion-pound companies that never invested in their workforce and these companies went out of business. This is in stark contrast to the multimillion pound companies who are known for investing in their workforce, and have remained strong financially, and even expanded as a company. Your most important asset is your workforce, and they must be made to feel that by receiving rewards for good service and longevity, as well as other such recognitions.

In this book, we may not be talking about multimillion pound companies, or hundreds of staff members being employed by you, but remember that your staff and your customers are your clients, and they must always be made to feel special. Even if you do it just for the recommendation, it would be worth it.

Chapter 34
Social Media

Social Media is one of the most effective ways to promote your product or service, and it is also cost effective. Social Media includes many different online tools. You have the internet, and emails, and both can be used via your smartphone, you can also use social media to direct your marketing campaign.

There are many ways to follow up people that have contacted you, whether it be through email, internet or by telephone. You can email customers once a week and respond to any queries. You can use Facebook to target specific customers, and the good thing about social networks is that you can display different testimonies of people, that have already experienced your product or service, which then shows people how good you are.

There is also conference calling, video calling, and webinars, where you can speak to people anywhere in the world and look at them while you are speaking to them. You could do it on a screen in an office or internet café, or from your home if you have the internet.

There are also ways you can advertise through pay per click, so when potential customers visit your website, you only pay if they click through. It is a lot more cost effective than advertising in daily newspapers, and weekly or monthly magazines, radio, or on TV. On the internet there are things such as display advertising, where you can display your product, or service across someone else's website.

Using the internet to advertise is a way to expand your geographical area. You can be one person sat in a small office in England, but you can be open to the world through the internet.

You can use different levels of marketing on the internet, such as advertising premium priced versions of what you do or sell. You can also advertise other companies, or self-employed people, and charge them for that. Putting a video online providing more detail about what you are selling can be very effective.

Through social media you can capture all aspects of your marketing. You can use WhatsApp and send a picture, and that could be your brochure or your business card. You could use Snapchat to say something different every day or every week. You could have a page on your own website, where you ask for referrals, or you could offer people rewards, or money, for giving you referrals, so the list goes on.

Try to use all the social media platforms available to get your personality out there, so people can see what kind of person you are, the person behind the brand of the business, product, or service.

Advertising agencies have always been incredibly good but are also very expensive. If you have just started your own business and are going to be earning approximately the average annual income, then maybe using an advertising agency would not be suitable for you. Depending on what you are doing, you could get teams of people to do it, or even a third party.

Snapchat allows you to take pictures with different types of filters, frames, stickers, colours, and text. You can send messages, videos, and pictures, on your mobile phone, to your friends but once you send the picture, video, or message it will disappear within seconds.

Snapchat also allows you to make a story so everyone on your friends list can see it, or you can make it public worldwide, but your story will only last for 24 hours. If you have your mobile phone location turned on, and your friends have their location on too, you can access Snap maps which will show you a map, and you will see where they are in the world. Snapchat allows you to make audio and video calls. You can also add your business website link, YouTube, or blogs.

Facebook allows you to have a personal page or a business page. With Facebook you can upload pictures, videos and a biography about yourself, or your business to let your friends on Facebook know more about you or the business you are promoting. You can also set reminders and events whilst tagging people on them. You can add maps to your profile to allow people to see where you are. Facebook allows you to upload your status to let people know what you are up to or if you have something on your mind you want to share. You can share links, photos, events, and you can also sell items, plus join all sort of groups. Facebook now allows you to make calls and screen live videos.

Instagram is a social media page which allows you to upload as many pictures or videos as you want, where you can use different filters to make pictures look better or different. Instagram allows you to have followers, and for you to follow other people, so people can see your photos, like them, save them and write comments under the picture. If you post a picture of you and some friends, you can tag them in it, so they know you have uploaded a photo with them in it. This can also be used to promote products or events for your business.

A lot of people use Instagram to promote their business page. Instagram has now got a storyline, so you can add a story for everyone to see but this will disappear after 24 hours. Instagram also allows you to follow celebrities, to keep up to date with your favourite people, places, and trends.

Twitter allows you to write a status update, show an image, link to a blog or reply to other peoples' 'tweets'. You can also share information you find on the internet that you know your customers might be interested in. A lot of businesspeople have twitter, which they use to promote a business or product or sell items. Twitter allows you to post pictures, and link to hash tags so that you can contribute to a current topic relevant to your audience.

LinkedIn is a social networking website aimed at connecting business professionals, employers, employees, and groups. People use it to advertise themselves and their professional experience, and to link with likeminded individuals. It is a great way to promote your business by using this free platform to network in your chosen industry. If your needs change you can also access their premium service for a regular fee.

Pinterest, like all the other social media platforms, can be used on the web and via mobile applications. Users display images known as pins on a pin board. You can upload, save, sort, and manage your images to have different collections.

All the social media applications mentioned here can be used for pleasure, for business or both. Different businesses are drawn to certain media, and many customers prefer to hang out where they are learning or being entertained. Your task is to find out where your potential customers are online, and how you can turn them into customers.

Chapter 35
Next Step

Next Step was an organisation that I worked with some years ago. It was part of a government funded education charity that trained and developed the skills of unemployed people. I was contacted directly and asked to attend a meeting with the Chief Executive. At the meeting, the Chief Executive explained that the main reason for the meeting was that Next Step had received some funding to reach marginalised communities, and that they would like to hear my ideas in how they could reach those communities.

Organisations that are funded by the government normally complete returns (forms) to document how many people they have helped/assisted on an ongoing basis, showing that they have fulfilled the outcomes set out in the funding plan. Many organisations, especially if they are a part of larger organisations have the skills, expertise, and human resources to make applications for large sums of money and also become recipients of those large sums of money. These organisations are not always capable of reaching out to the desired population i.e. hard to reach groups, that they would like to have a positive impact on.

The Chief Executive, along with the managers of Next Step, attended the meeting and explained where I could help. They asked me to put together a proposal of how I could help them to achieve their targets reaching hard to reach groups. Within a week or so, I emailed them a proposal which stated that we would hire a venue at a location where I felt the marginalised groups would be happy going to. I considered that it was important for there to be refreshments, and that there would be enough promotion to have three events. I proposed to implement three one day events over a 3-month period, one per month.

I met with Next Step a few more times acknowledging that they had produced the publicity material as well as additional information that they wanted me to share with our guests. They also required me to speak about what they had to offer. The Next Step office was in Reading town centre, in a location easy to get to however people were not getting there in numbers. As a result, we put together a plan based on my proposal. The payment for my time was agreed and it was a win-win situation for all. We had post-event meetings and the outcome was that Next Step had increased reach into the communities they wanted to target. They also had many more people visiting their offices that they were giving advice to.

I was introduced to another lady that ran an organisation called InBiz. InBiz was set up to work with the long term unemployed, to help them into self-employment. InBiz encompassed well-meaning people who were running the business.

Subsequently, I met with a lady and a gentleman that were managing the business in the Berkshire area. They had a contract with the Department of Employment. Similarly, to Next Step, InBiz had target numbers to reach so we carried out a process in this organisation like the one carried out in Next Step. We set up meetings, and events inviting people from marginalised communities and even though it was a different organisation we were able to increase the community's participation. Now, with InBiz, I gave my time voluntarily as they were funded differently to Next Step. We set up a series of meetings that were for the community; I was linking the community with InBiz in my own time as a part of giving back to the community.

A further example of being called upon to support the community, was when a new organisation was being formed to support new and existing community enterprises. The organisation was called Social Enterprise Berkshire. Again, this was an organisation that had received some funding to work with communities across the Berkshire area.

A Social Enterprise is similar to a profit-making company. However, it is set up so that it is not for personal profit. So, any money that it might make which could be a profit, or surplus in this case, must either be used in the business or reinvested into the community.

When Social Enterprise Berkshire was set up, I was asked if I could meet with the lady that was managing it at the time. I met with her and some of her other colleagues and we had a discussion on how best to reach marginalised communities. This is another organisation that I assisted voluntarily without asking them for anything in return for my time. As with all the organisations that I have worked with, I met some great people, and we put one group of people in contact with another group.

People tend to be used to a community group, knowing what volunteering is and what a charity is, however sometimes people were not clear about what a social enterprise was or what it meant being 'not for profit'.

This meant that I could meet with potential clients of the organisation and brief them with what a social enterprise is or what it does. I would then take them to meet with Social Enterprise Berkshire. I did this because some of us in the community have the responsibility to use our contacts to make sure we connect people with others they might not necessarily have met otherwise. In the same way that we connect people, or people connect people, as brokers or introducers, and get paid for it in the private sector. The difference here is that some of us will go that extra mile to connect people just for the sake of doing it voluntarily.

Therefore, being in business, being self-employed, and being very connected to the community, has many more benefits than just being self-employed and being external to the community. As well as this, what I was able to do with this organisation was introduce them to community groups that had members they could talk to, to increase their reach. While these events were going on.

All these roles and opportunities would not have been available to me if I had been in full time employment. Firstly, I would have had to focus on my employment, and the weekends where I would normally have time off, would be spent with my family. So, the advent of self-employment and managing your own time can give you a lot more flexibility to help other people and become involved with other organisations whilst linking people and organisations to one another.

Chapter 36
No Man is an Island

A view of mine that I hold onto dearly is that in order to have a leading team to reach your goals, you must first seek a good team leader to build a team that shares your values.

The team created must be led by a strong person who is both positive and self-assured. With this knowledge as I looked through all my contacts, I thought of a person whom I have known for many years who fitted the description of team leader. This individual and I had grown apart over the years as we both pursued our different chosen careers; he chose sales and I ended up an entrepreneur.

From time to time, we would see each other and use that opportunity to have a quick catch up on what both we and our mutual friends have been up to. Then, we would say our goodbyes and knew we may not reunite until we bump into one another a year or so down the line. Despite this, in case we need to talk, we both have each other's mobile phone numbers.

Consistently at the back of my mind is the view that if you want something done you need to find the best person for the job and do it. As a result, it was time to phone a friend. A friend that I have known for multiple years and have always had a lot of respect for. I contacted this friend and said to him "I'd like to take you out for a meal as I want to speak to you about an idea I have, whilst also catching up on the old times".

For over two years, I had been working on a business concept; a discount card which my friend had been involved. To add, my friend is exceptionally good at his profession and has even won awards constantly moving from place to place because he was always surpassing targets. Moreover, when I had finished explaining the concept to him, I was feeling really upbeat about it because I knew he had the skills and experience necessary to be my leading person.

Then, just before I offered the opportunity to him to gain his viewpoint, he said something that really took me back. He said "Keith you have a great idea however, those kinds of ideas are too big for the likes of us, it's more suited for people like Richard Branson. Someone like him needs to run something like that".

At this point, my friend had no idea that I was going to offer him a major role in my new company. After we finished our meal, we said our goodbyes and parted. I must admit I was bewildered although, I learned a valuable lesson.

However much you may believe in yourself, however much you may believe in your ability, however much you might believe in someone else's ability and success, if you are going to bring them on board to work with you especially as a leading light in your company or organisation they must also share that similar belief to you.

Two things struck me, one was if I took him on board would he believe in himself if he started off not believing in me and my ability? Secondly, if he does not believe in me and my ability then it may not work. Yet, we can achieve if first we believe.

The first part of this chapter illustrates the mental processes some entrepreneurs possess. The thought that we cannot go it alone and no matter how many people we work with, we must not give up. The reason being, we may not have chosen the right person and so we must try again but cannot do it on our own as no man is an island.

The second part of this chapter is about a different type of working together. It takes place in a community setting where for almost twenty years, I shadowed a man to learn about leading community groups. In my eyes, this man is a political heavyweight, a community champion, a leader, and a friend. Earlier on in my book, I have written about my business mentor and continued to write about some of the people that first involved me in community work. But what I am about to mention is someone I began to shadow around ten years after I had established myself as an entrepreneur.

Joe. Someone that inspired me to become involved in community matters, community groups and charities more seriously including becoming chairman of organisations over the last twenty years. Far too often we forget to mention whose shoulders we stand on, because many of us quite rightly mention parents as our role models.

Some of us even have our own children, pop stars, rock stars, R&B stars, actors and sports personnel as our role models. However, it is not often that I've come across an individual who has the wealth of knowledge Joe has, including being the first ever BME elected County Councillor to Berkshire County Council. No one can take away being the first. Years after meeting Joe, I referred to my father and a few of my cousins to which he told me he knew my family. He continued to say that about 35 years or so ago it was my father that brought him to Reading from the airport when Joe first arrived in England.

Ultimately, I was working on committees being mentored by Joe who is excellent in getting his point across, has made history and paved the way. He can articulate his journey through politics and beyond and is a proud family man. Joe is someone I will be forever indebted to, regarding the skills and knowledge he has transferred to me. I gained Joe as my mentor some 10 years before writing this book and even though it was in no official capacity he has been more of an effective mentor than I could have ever wished for and I want to remind people that no man is an island, no man stands alone.

SLOW DOWN

CHILD
CROS

map
authority

fresh and innovative approach to personal and community development

Mary Seacole Day Nursery
& Family Support Unit

Ofsted Registered

ITION
RIES MUST
EED DIRECTLY INTO
ICTLY NO
THIS AREA

Apollo Youth Club

Est. 1972

Ofsted registered

berkshire phab

Chapter 37
MAPP Centre

Reading, Berkshire, has a close-knit community, and being active in business, and community work, as well as producing popular community magazines, I was often approached and invited to become involved in local community organisations.

One such organisation was the MAP Partnership; a partnership of three organisations providing excellent community services. I had known about the organisations for a while and knew some of the people involved in running them, as well as some of the service users and clients. I went along to a few of the committee meetings, met with trustees and answered the call when I was nominated and subsequently elected as Chairperson, which I have been so far, for approximately four years at the time of writing this book.

The MAP Partnership is the collective name for: 1. Mary Seacole Day Nursery, 2. Apollo Youth Club, and 3. PHAB. They became partners in order to provide a new purpose-built community facility at Mount Pleasant in the Katesgrove Ward of Reading, and MAPP was a product of that decision.

All three organisations have many years' experience as voluntary sector providers in their own right, and work in partnership to develop services which aim to improve access to work and training for the wider community. Moreover, the three lead partners are each registered with the Charities Commission, and the managing element of the centre, MAP Partnership, secured charitable status in September 2002 and is also a Company Limited by guarantee.

1. Mary Seacole provides a neighbourhood nursery.
2. Apollo provides out of school activities for young children.
3. PHAB provides an integrated drop-in for people with and without disabilities.

Due to the unique position of MAPP within the local community, along with the current activities provided by the Partners, it is the intention to extend and solidify the partners activities as an enabler, by establishing, organising and supporting activities linked to educational development within the local community.

The aim is to expand the weekend tutorial club to provide additional subject specific support to students who are in preparation for their examinations. As well as this, MAPP will strive to develop homework club activities geared to pupils of secondary school age.

Regarding daytime use, the centre is facilitated to ensure that all participants are given the opportunity to develop their knowledge, skills and self-confidence, in line with their interests, aspirations and abilities. Also ensuring that the individuals can adapt themselves to a changing world as well as the frequently and significantly changing and developing professions.

Evening use is directed at developing and organising programmes and activities which informs, educates and raises awareness about the contribution to scientific, economic, historical and cultural developments over the decades.

On the other hand, weekend use focuses on bringing people together to share experiences and participation in social and cultural activities and events which play a fundamental part in our everyday lives.

The following principles are at the core of the centre's operation:

Education – The future of our community is dependent on our young people being educated to engage in society as decision makers, intellectuals, entrepreneurs, and captains of industry, therefore an educational emphasis is placed at the core of the centre's operation.

Enterprise Development – Using the facility as an incubator to encourage the development of initiatives which results in valuable activities beneficial to individuals and the community, as well as reducing the dependency of the centre from relying on handouts from the state.

Cultural Awareness – The success of any community is dependent on the roots that are grown to provide strength and longevity, so activities undertaken would reflect this maxim, be a catalyst for development and serve as a beacon for further evolution.

The MAPP Centre is a dynamic organisation whose focus is on the educational advancement, entrepreneurial development, and cultural awareness of the community. This is central to the long-term success of the centre, resulting in ownership of ventures, participation in policy development and implementation and influencing strategic changes which have a beneficial effect on the local community.

In order to fully understand the ethos of the MAPP centre, I have listed the objectives as follows:

MAPP Centre Objectives:

a) To develop a facility which provides for the educational, entrepreneurial and self-help development of the community
b) To provide advice and guidance to users of the facility in respect of the provision of services which will assist the community to develop and prosper socially and economically.
c) To guarantee that the centre is maintained as a venue for activities which are beneficial to the well-being of the community.
d) To ensure programmes and activities which are beneficial for the needs of young people are developed and implemented.
e) To develop partnership arrangements with statutory and voluntary agencies in maximising

resources; this will be utilised to enhance self-help and enterprise development within the community.

f) To organise and provide services which are educationally beneficial and aids entrepreneurial development of the community.

g) To ensure the facility is used efficiently and effectively.

h) To develop close partnerships with users and the community which makes sense regarding business, as strong relationships enable us to work harmoniously in helping to develop sustainable communities and develop projects that help to improve quality of life.

The MAP Partnership being both a charity and a not for profit company, means that I am able to impart my numerous business skills, knowledge, and experiences into developing the centre. Many organisations of this type have historically struggled when they have been set up using funds that had been gained by a type of community grant. Most of the businesses that I have been involved in over the years have been built by myself from scratch with no grants or loans.

Navigating through the maze of obstacles presented to businesses, mirror that of those presented to community groups. Conversely, since becoming Chairperson, I have brought onboard some new trustees/directors, and together we are in the process of making the MAP Partnership more financially sustainable in the long term.

Chapter 38
Lemon Hall

My parents were both born in a small rural village in St Catherine, Jamaica, called Lemon Hall. There was no running water and no electricity, and a hole within a wooden shed like building outside, for a toilet.

Both my mother's and father's families lived in Lemon Hall. Both families ran very small grocery shops around five minutes away from each other, and these shops served the village. There were no cars in the village, as there were no roads, and it was about a two mile walk uphill in forest like terrain to get to the main road. From the main road, cars and buses would use this route to get children to school, to go to the market, post office, doctors or to take you out of the area i.e. to the larger cities and the airport.

Whilst I was in Jamaica, I rode a donkey for the first time. It was both scary and exciting at the same time. It was so different to England and what I was already used to. The patois (broken English spoken in Jamaica) that most people spoke was so strong that I had to ask my father to sometimes translate what was being said for me to understand, however the thing I remember the most was the heat and the way people were so friendly. They did not have much in the way of material things however they loved singing, dancing, and loved visitors.

Shortly after my father came to England from Lemon Hall, which he did to earn some money and make a way for his fiancée to come over, he was able to send enough money for my mother to come over to England, and then a couple of years later they got married.

In 1960s Jamaica, people wanted to go to England, Canada or America in order to better their lives. So, people would really work hard towards saving to go to those countries, and some parents would even put some money together so their children could be sent abroad to have what they thought were better opportunities in life.

I remember my father telling me that at the time when he came over to England to better his life, he had to work for three months and save every penny to afford the air ticket to come over.

Now, as I write this book, many people earning the average wage, if they travelled at the right time of year in the UK, could get a return flight to Jamaica working for only one week.

When we try to measure the difference between then and now, comparing whether you are wealthy or poor. One of the measurements could be that if you do the same thing from different sides of the globe to see how much effort you must put in to achieve the same amount i.e. value in monetary terms.

My father and I visited Jamaica when I was fourteen years old. He told me that the village of Lemon Hall had not really changed since he left Jamaica.

Going to Jamaica was the first time I flew on an aeroplane. I had never realised how large a 747 jumbo jet was until I caught sight of the plane from close proximity. The flight lasted for about eight hours.

Once we landed in Jamaica, there were many people at the airport trying to get us to come into their taxis. There was a lot of wrestling for our attention however we had one of our cousins collect us and I remember this long, long drive for about an hour and half until we got to the place where I would eventually stay for the remainder of time we stayed in Jamaica.

We walked down a hill and it was quite rocky and uneven, there was sugar cane, mangoes, coconuts and banana trees growing along the sides of the pathway. There were lots of different fruits and they smelt really nice and fresh. Eventually we got to this small wooden house and my father explained that it was where his parents lived, and where we would be staying whilst visiting Jamaica.

The house was built a few feet off the ground, it was on kind of like stilts, and in the house, there was about four rooms. I remember at the time that there was no television, but there was a radio.

One night at the weekend, my dad had to go into town, which meant it was a trek up the hill, catching a bus for about thirty minutes or so, then getting to the main road and catching another bus, and then another couple of hours into town, so he decided he was going to stay at his sisters and then come back the next day.

I was therefore left to sleep in a room on my own with a little candle lamp that you had to light, so it had a little flame. The memory that sticks with me was when I saw a scorpion on the wall a few feet above my head. I don't believe that I've ever been so frightened in my life. I don't think I slept, I think I just watched the scorpion all night, but it didn't harm me, and I told my father when he came back the next day, and he said it was nothing to worry about.

Sometimes we would take the exceedingly long walk up to the top of the hill and we would go on bus rides to visit other family members. On one occasion we even went to Linstead market, which is kind of a world-famous market in Jamaica where you can buy ackee, saltfish, fruits and vegetables.

Ackee is a fruit, and the national fruit of Jamaica. The other thing quite different was as you would be driving down a main road, you would pass a large sound system blasting out reggae music, with massive speaker boxes the size of wardrobes, with the bass and treble very loud, and nobody minding the noise.

People would walk past and might even dance for a while and then continue walking. The culture was quite different, and in the town, people were occasionally begging which was something else I was not used to. The buses and taxis would always be overfilled, whereas in England when you get in a car there may be four of you at the time, or maybe even five of you. Unless you had a mini bus where maybe 11 or 12 of you had a seat, however in Jamaica the cars for four or five people would have maybe eight or nine passengers, and in the buses not only did they have people on the buses, it was packed but still they would have animals, like chickens on their lap or over above the rail.

Those experiences were really different to what I had been used to but after a while it was okay and I realised that's the way people lived and I can say I really did enjoy my visit to Jamaica, including my first long haul flight, and meeting my extended family.

Synopsis

My Business journey would not be complete without me adding certain aspects of the things that have happened to me along the way.

In *leadership*, if you are the head of a company you need to show strong leadership, you cannot be seen to be weak. You need to ensure that you have what it takes to carry the company on your shoulders.

It is interesting because when I look back and I think of those stories that my mother and father used to tell me about the issues and challenges I used to give them, and that is why I see myself as a *problem child*. I am not sure what and how that contributed to my mindset, but I think that *your mindset* really has a lot of elements and facets to it.

I was a problem pupil to my teachers, and I think because of that I wanted to prove that I could excel in something and that is how I became the record holder in the one hundred metre sprint at school all those years ago...*And the Winner is*...

As for the DJ business *Frogs and Trogs*, I recall what fun times we had as we entered adulthood.

I learned to play guitar at school and after word got around, I was called and asked to audition for a new band called *Urban Warrior*. I ended up performing in the band playing bass guitar and we toured several countries. This was another taste of being involved in business as we would charge for each of our performances.

Then from moving from *job to job*, having five jobs with five different employers in my first year after leaving school, which made me realise that I was going to have to make some big adjustments to be able to conform to some degree in society.

To pay my bills I had to find work as I was on benefits, so I got a temporary job at Mars, which is an International chocolate factory. I always saw this job as temporary, but my parents felt I should have stayed on because it was a steady income, however it just was not for me. *From Mars to Benefits* tells the tale of my short-lived Twix nightmare.

It was not too long before I believed I was *unemployable*, but to relieve some of the underlying anger and aggression I was feeling, I continued to be involved in *contact sports*. It was the boxing, karate, and rugby that enabled me to really let off some steam.

I then embarked upon *employing myself* and that was a noticeably big step within itself.

Kensington and Maidenhead: If you go back many years and then you fast forward, you will see that property is something where if you had money that you had invested in property, and you have left it for long enough, those property prices will rise, and they are solid investments.

As we all know people are living longer, and care homes like *Seville Lodge* are sometimes the best place for people to live to ensure that they have regular care if they are on their own or if their partner, husband, or wife are unable to care for them.

As for mentoring, the fact that I was a *mentee to mentor*, and someone was able to mentor me in business, made me then want to get involved in mentoring. I did it in a more structured way by being trained by a mentoring organisation. In terms of job satisfaction, it was really something that I am glad I embarked upon.

To buy cars, especially if they are newer cars, they would be bought using a finance facility that we provided through *Capital Direct*.

Training professionals, such as Senior Police Officers who are training their junior officers '*Train the Trainer*'. I never thought I would have become a freelance trainer in community relations. As a self-employed person opportunity can arise at any time. Be prepared to grab them with both hands.

My Magazine *Urban News* was a way to let people know of the colourful community that we all belong to. We highlighted community achievements in print, and community leaders.

I continued being involved in different voluntary groups and then decided to set up *The Big Debate*, which is a 'question time' style panel, it was a chance for the forgotten communities to get together and speak to the local authorities and tell them their views and get the opportunity to have an input into that process.

Nesta Care was a business where we provided care, domiciliary care and supported living for the elderly and adults with disabilities. Again, you need to ensure that you are doing it properly and within the law.

I have realised that it does not matter what you do, how you do it, when you do it, why you do it and where you do it, there will always be naysayers, the people that are negative about what you are doing. There will always be people that want to put a dampener on everything, however you need to continue to rise above them and prove them wrong and show them that there are some positives – *avoiding naysayers*.

It's important to research the kind of business you want to do, and by speaking to people already in that sector. *Market Research* is key, however obtaining information from organisations is another challenge but it was something that I had to embark upon to become an effective businessperson. In some ways when you start a business and it does not work out the way you thought it would, you think it is impossible, but you must get up, brush yourself off and continue.

A *Mission Statement* is something you can put together to guide you through the maze of self-employment. It can assist in planning how to get new customers and help to navigate you through the maze of setting up your business. Your mission statement can work wonders for the direction of your business.

We often see people from minority communities setting up businesses in minority areas hoping that those customers will buy their products and services and make them remarkably successful. When you are in a country that has a 90% majority and 10% is the minority, sometimes that *minority mentality* ideology does backfire.

Never underestimate the power of your *business location*. Of course, it depends on what type of business you are in. It is good to get to know the other people and businesses in your location. The culture of the area, and the movers and shakers, can be invaluable to getting and understanding your new surroundings.

Rules and regulations are probably the most fundamental aspect of a business that you need to get right when *starting up*. You need to ensure that you have all the right legal processes and licenses if required.

In terms of *marketing and communication*, people need to know who you are, they need to know where you are, and you need to continue to let them know by communicating to them in many ways and forms.

Snakes and Ladders may be a game, but it is also a game of real life. You might go down a snake depending on the move you make and sometimes you might get to go up a ladder depending on the throw of the dice. Most of us should want to be going up more ladders, we do not want to be going down too many snakes.

The *pricing* of your product or service must be right, it cannot be too low, or too high and it is important to look at comparable prices just to make sure that you are pitching your pricing right. And then there is *getting paid*, sometimes you provide a service and then you get paid afterwards, you need to make sure you get paid and you have processes in place to make sure that happens.

You may feel that you have little control over the circumstances that you are in, and you may go as far as attributing it to someone else or something else. All I am saying is that if you have put on unwanted weight – *don't blame the fridge*. If your business is not going well don't blame the weather.

The *continued learning* aspect of the book is to let you know that you will not know everything, and you will never know everything. Times are changing, so the more you can keep learning the more you will know, and as the saying goes 'knowledge is power', *know what you don't know*.

As for *managing people*, I am not cut out for that, I believe I suffer from transference where other people's problems become my problems because I want to kind of heal the world, so to speak.

Social Media is moving extremely fast and you must keep up to date with it. However if you are not personally a technical person, you should make sure you have staff that are, and that can keep you up to speed.

Education and business each work side by side and can be highly effective. *Next Step* was such an organisation supporting unemployed people and helping them through education. One to one working is a positive way of helping people get on with their lives.

No Man is an Island explains that no one person is everything to a business. We are all interdependent, we depend on each other to start and grow a business. The key aspect is to make sure you team up with people that have the correct skills that can complement one another and learn from each other.

Nurseries for children, day centres for people with disabilities, and after school and holiday clubs, are the backbone of any aspiring society. Without such support services the society we live in will ultimately break down. The *MAPP Centre* provides a home for such charities, which are essential for families with young children, and carers.

Lemon Hall is the tiny village is St. Catherine, Jamaica where my parents and their parents before them were born and grew up. Although there was no electricity, and running water, they prospered through a strong community spirit and love for each other. They say it takes a village to raise a child. Lemon Hall is a true example.

I would like us to spare a thought for those loved ones that we may have lost along the way, they may not be here physically, but we feel them spiritually. The fact that we cannot see and touch them, does not mean we love them any less, in many ways we yearn for them and in many ways, we love them even more.

Hall of Cards showcases examples of business cards that I have received over the years. A business card is a very cost-effective way of marketing your business.

Postscript

Although my journey is unique, many of the experiences shared in this book can happen to anyone. This is not a conventional business book, but it gives you great insight into the thinking and challenges of an entrepreneur.

Looking back at my business experiences has been amazing, as so much has happened in a little over thirty years. We often think we do not have enough time, however all our small activities can add up to something substantial.

I have come to appreciate what different people bring into my life. In business, as well as my community life, people are our most valuable assets, yet we often overlook this. I have learnt lessons from children, adults, elderly, the rich and poor, although many times without realising it.

As I delved into writing this book, I found my memories becoming more vivid. Things I have not thought of for years, have come back to me in a new way.

At times, being in business can feel lonely, but it does not need to be that way. There are business communities throughout the country.

I conclude by sharing with you where I am now in business. I am running Devana Care, a health and social care business, and whilst the care business is taking up most of my time, I am also running a car finance brokerage called Mobay Autos, and I am looking to launch a discount card company, that I have been working on over the past three years, crossing the T's, and dotting the I's. It is all about getting the right team, because as they say, 'teamwork makes the dream work'.

I hope this book will have a positive impact on your endeavours, and that you enjoy sharing it with others in your network.

If you would like further information, please visit www. mineyourbusiness.co.uk

Keith Seville

Mine Your Business: Questions and Answers with Author, Keith Seville

What is Mine Your Business about?

– Mine Your Business is a business book that I put together, that describes my journey through self-employment, it begins from when I was at school selling sweets in the playground, right up to when I started hiring and firing people and beyond.

What inspired you to write Mine Your Business?

– The inspiration came from the many people continuously asking me questions about business, being in business, and what it is like to be in business. People say they would like to start their own business, and wonder what my journey was like, and if they started their own business, would they have similar ups and downs.

I hear people talking about the different people that they have met, multi-millionaires in business, people that are just getting through, people that have failed in business, people that have succeeded. So, because of all those reasons, I thought it was time to share.

Did your professional background help in the writing of Mine Your Business?

– Well my professional background is as an entrepreneur, although I do have further education postgraduate qualifications in teaching, and business management. I do think that along the way my different training has helped me, and sometimes even when I don't think it has, it has when I've looked back.

How did you get involved with working for yourself?

– I started working for myself after I left school; I had a few jobs that just didn't seem to suit me, and I didn't seem to suit them, so I felt that working for myself would be an alternative to working for someone else.

How did you decide what information was crucial to include in Mine Your Business?

– When I first started writing this book, I was planning to write it just about my business experiences, but a colleague of mine, a fellow author, advised me that maybe I should put some of my own life experiences in the book, that aren't directly involved with me being in business, however they are in some way connected.

Are you working on any current business projects?

– Being an entrepreneur, you tend to always be working on new projects, and I am working on some projects at the moment. I am working on a health and social care business, a motor vehicle finance brokerage, a building project, and I intend to launch a discount card company.

What are the most common struggles that you face in business?

– The most common struggle I face in business is the most common struggle that I think many people face, which is finance. You can't really open a business without pouring money into it, and if you want to borrow the money, people don't want to lend it to you because they haven't seen your proven success, and if you use your savings, then a lot of times it means that you can't pay your own bills, so money has always been the real challenge in running your own business.

Do you believe we need to be more informed about self-employment?

– Absolutely. There are many people I've met, that working for somebody else just doesn't fit them, but they don't have the know how, in order to work for themselves, so I think that if people were more in tune with working for themselves, from a real grass roots level, rather than starting up to be multi-millionaires in a short time, then they can start slow, build up, and have the information that they really need to succeed and prosper.

Which writers inspire you?

– The writers that inspire me aren't so much writers by name so to speak, however they are more writers in terms of genre for instance, personal development books like 'Unlimited Power' by Anthony Robbins, 'The 7 habits of highly effective people' by Stephen R. Covey, and 'The Road Less Travelled' by M. Scott Peck. I also enjoy reading autobiographies of businesspeople, I've read a few of those, and they've inspired me.

What are you currently reading?

– I'm currently not reading any specific book, it's not something that I've been doing recently, as I've spent the last couple of years working on writing my own. I have read this book, over and over to make sure it is right. So, what I'm currently reading is 'Mine Your Business'.

Do you have any advice for aspiring businesspeople?

– My advice for aspiring businesspeople is to go where your heart takes you and take the plunge. If you want to start a business, see what information you can find out about it, speak to whoever you need to speak to about it, find information, whether it's on the internet, or through books or other people that have done business in a similar field that you want to go in, and go for it - if you never do it, you would never know how it would have gone.

What would you say to someone who asks whether they should write their own book?

This is a question that I have been asked more than any other question since my book was published. The answer will always be yes, yes, go for it, especially if its about your own experiences. The experience can be insurmountable and once it is done it can never be undone. You will unearth things that you had long forgotten, some good, some bad, however all important.

Our Monica

Monica Seville lost her battle against Motor Neurone Disease on 9th October 2016, aged 54, at Royal Berkshire Hospital. Monica who had been a manager in the caring profession for over 25 years, was a proud mother of two daughters and a grandmother of two.

Earlier on in 2015, Monica wrote the article below on her Eye Gaze machine. Just using her eyes to scroll through the alphabet as she was unable to use her hands anymore.

My name is Monica, I was diagnosed with M.N.D. (Motor Neurone Disease) on the 31st July 2013; Can you imagine when we got the news, my world came crashing down around me it was the worst day of my life and my family's lives. I still can't believe this has happened to me. I have an amazing family and carers, they keep me going. I feel very blessed to still be alive today.

My family keep me going I see them every day, they take it in turns to come and see me, they have their own special day to visit, and they always come, they never miss a day, it is really nice spending time with them individually.

I have had M.N.D. for three and a half years, and the first thing I noticed was I started limping, and then I started falling over. Then my right hand started twitching, and as the days, weeks and months went by I became progressively worse and the only part of my body I could move is my head and my thumb on my left hand, but I am so grateful to be alive.

I went into hospital about six months ago with breathing problems, they told my family I would not make it through the night, my family were distraught, and the doctors did not want to give me any oxygen but my mum begged them to give me the oxygen and so they did. Mum said to the doctors it is not up to us to say when my daughter will die, it's up to the bigger man, I am still here, and I don't intend on going anywhere for a long time.

Me, my family and my carers will continue to fight this war until we win this battle. I would not wish this terrible disease on my worst enemy. I am very lucky to have the carers I have; they will do anything for me, I do have to pull them up sometimes, they forget I was a manager for 25 years in the caring field. There is no pulling the wool over my eyes; On a whole they are lovely girls. I tend to go for younger carers because they always have a story to tell, and the stories are always very interesting, and I look forward to hearing them.

My carers come from a company called Devana Care, they are really good to me, and they always have my best interest at heart. They always listen to what I have to say, and they act on it. I will never change care agencies.

M.N.D. stands for MOTOR NEURONE DISEASE, there are four types, the one I have is called A.L.S. which is where the muscles in your body start dying, which leaves you feeling very weak and unable to move, it is such a terrible disease and one of the worse things about this illness is when you have to wear a face mask to help with your breathing, that bit of it is ok, the only thing is no-one can understand you when you're wearing the mask. It is so difficult for anyone to understand me, I get so frustrated about it, but I manage to keep my cool. It is not anyone's fault and it is really hard watching my carers and family doing my housework, I was so house proud.

At least I can talk or use my computer to communicate with everyone. I know I am lucky to be alive, and to be able to talk and eat, I feel very blessed, so thank you guys for all your blessings. I eat and drink very well, the only thing is I have to remove my mask often when I'm eating and when I'm having my medication. I try not to think about it too much otherwise I will get upset. I just take each day as it comes and thank God I'm alive. What I will say though is that I have met some amazing people since I became ill. I would not have met them if I did not have this dreadful illness, so there are some positive things about this illness.

Another awful thing about this illness is that it is hard for you to hold a conversation because of my mask, it is so difficult, but again I am not going to give up, no matter what is thrown at me.

I just want to mention a few people who have had a major impact on my life, first the most amazing woman in the world, who happens to be my mum. If it was not for my mum, I would not have had those amazing holidays abroad so thanks mum. Also thank you for being you, I love you unconditionally.

I want to say a few things about my brother Keith Seville; what an incredible man. Keith has always been the one to take me to all my hospital and doctor appointments, there was never a day where Keith could not take me, I always came first, Keith would change whatever appointments he had to take me where I needed to go thank you again Keith for what you have done for me and my family, I love you from the bottom of my heart, I know you will keep up the good work. Me and Keith have always been very close, but since I became ill we have become even more closer, even though I thought we could not become any more closer. I love you bro.

Now about my wonderful daughters, I have two amazing daughters, Natalie and Shona. We have always been very close, they have been my rock, they are with me most days, they are so strong, they get that from me, but I know deep down inside they are struggling to come to terms with the fact they are going to lose their mum, but we don't talk about that, only positive things. They keep me going bless them, I love you girls more than you will ever know.

I have been blessed with two amazing granddaughters, Jada and Saraeya, we are very close, and I see them all the time. When I was driving, I used to look forward to picking them up at the weekends, but now they're old enough to come and see me on their own, which is so nice, they are one of the reasons I have to keep going - just stay as sweet as you are girls, nanny loves you very much.

Now for the rest of my family, I want to thank you all from the bottom of my heart for all the support you have given me, you have all been amazing, you are my soldiers and we will keep fighting this dreadful war together. I love you all like cooked food.

If I had to sum up this illness, it's like I have committed this dreadful crime and now I am being punished for it. It's like being behind bars in prison, watching the world go by, and there is nothing I can do about it. I hope one day soon, they will find a cure for this dreadful disease, I would not wish this on my worst enemy. Whatever plans you all have, take it from me, just do it, because you don't know what's around the corner, there is no warning.

I thank God for my family and carers, you're more like family so thank you again for keeping me looking this good. I thank you God for giving me the strength to carry on.

Kindest regards
Monica Seville
p.s. I hope you all enjoyed reading my article as much as I enjoyed writing it. Much love!

About the Author

Keith Seville is a first-time author, serial entrepreneur, and magazine publisher.

He started his first business as a teenager, and has set up and operated many businesses, for more than 30 years.

Keith has set up businesses in property, mobile phones, financial services, and health and social care. Keith has also successfully published two magazine titles.

In the year 2002, he won a Millennium award for the first magazine he published in 2000 called Urban News. He has also written a training course entitled 'An introduction to self-employment'.

Keith has been the Chairman of many voluntary organisations including registered charities, and he set up Urban UK Network in 2003. He is a trained mentor and is also the founder and host of The Big Debate since 2009, which has included the leaders of the local main political parties, joining him on a panel with business and community leaders.

Keith holds a postgraduate qualification in Management from Buckingham Chiltern University UK, another postgraduate qualification in Further Education Teaching from Thames Valley University UK. Keith is also a Common Purpose Graduate.

HALL
of
CARDS

Alagappa Jeganathan
Chairperson

45 Grosvenor Road
St Albans
Hertfordshire AL1 3AW
United Kingdom
Web www.mbn.org.uk

Tel: 020 8447 1075
Mobile: 07720 374962
E-mail: jcclondon@aol.com

NAVAL & MILITARY CLUB
The In & Out

Ian Gregory
Club Secretary

No. 4, St. James's Square, London SW1Y 4JU
Tel: 020 7827 5757 Direct Line: 020 7827 5734 Fax: 020 7827 5740
Email: ian.gregory@navalandmilitaryclub.co.uk
www.navalandmilitaryclub.co.uk

Ian A. Akers PhD
Regional Co-ordinator, South East

Mentoring+
Befriending
Foundation
South East

Mentoring and Befriending Foundation,
220 Vale Road,
Tonbridge,
Kent,
TN9 1SP

Tel: 01732 373099
Mobile: 07971 199424
Fax: 01732 373001
Email: ian.akers@mandbf.org.uk
Website: www.mandbf.org.uk

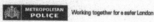

NICHOLS EMPLOYMENT AGENCY

Joy Nichols
Director

95 Goldhawk Road
Shepherd's Bush
London
W12 8EG

Tel: 0208 746 4800
Fax: 0208 743 0263
j.nichols@nichols-agency.co.uk
www.nichols-agency.co.uk

METROPOLITAN POLICE   Working together for a safer London

Vanessa Nicholls
Director Strategy
Room 812
New Scotland Yard
London SW1 0BG

Tel: 020 7230 2793
email: vanessa.nicholls@met.police.uk

Jak Babuela-Dodd - Chair

General enquiries: 0800 093 0400
Admin enquiries: 020 692 4880 • Fax: 020 692 4881
120-126 High Road, London NW6 4HY
Email: info@nubianjak.com

MILTON GORDON & Co.
INDEPENDENT FINANCIAL ADVISER

Milton Gordon
MIFP. MLIA (dip)

33 Hart Street, Henley-On-Thames, Oxon, RO9 2AR
Tel. 01491-578999 Fax. 01491-578003

P E N N   L E G A L

Solicitors and Commissioners for Oaths

Zafar Ali M.A (Oxon)

Gainsborough House, 17-23 High Street, Slough, Berkshire, SL1 1DY.
Telephone: 0870 043 4275 Fax: 0870 043 4276
Web: www.pennlegal.co.uk Email: zafar.ali@pennlegal.co.uk

nameless uk digital media & marketing

Jaya Chakrabarti managing director
e: jaya@nameless-uk.com   m: +44 (0)7967 190406
www.nameless-uk.com

Mary Shek
Arts Council England, South East, Sovereign House, Church Street
Brighton BN1 1RA
Phone: 0845 300 6200 Direct: 44 (0)1273 763028 Mobile: 07739 946142
Fax: 0870 242 1257 Textphone: 44 (0)1273 710659
Email: mary.shek@artscouncil.org.uk www.artscouncil.org.uk

Shona King
SALES MANAGER

Thames Valley Chamber of Commerce Group
467 Malton Avenue • Slough • Berkshire • SL1 4QU
Direct Tel: 01753 870608 Fax: 01753 870609 Mobile: 07843 346468
Email: shonaking@thamesvalleychamber.co.uk
www.thamesvalleychamber.co.uk

Steve Ball
Education Director

Direct Line: +44 (0)121 245 2091
Mobile: +44 (0)7974 138 401
Email: steve.ball@birmingham-rep.co.uk

Birmingham Repertory Theatre Ltd, Centenary Square, Broad Street, Birmingham B1 2EP
Administration +44 (0)121 245 2000   Facsimile +44 (0)121 245 2100
Box Office +44 (0)121 236 4455   www.birmingham-rep.co.uk

 SOCURE LIMITED

Castle Hill House
Castle Hill
Windsor
Berkshire SL4 1PD

Dr. Sylvia Chukwuemeka MBBS,
FRSH, FIMS (Dip IMS), MIHPE

Stress Management Consultant

Telephone: 01753 839384
Fax: 01753 842862
Email: info@socure.com
www.socure.com

SOCURE ●●○○○

Suzanna Taverne

35 Camden Square
London NW1 9XA

T   020 7284 2421
M   07957 380 658
E   taverne@vlessing.com

 SALON STRATEGIES
...give your business a makeover!

Anne Long-Murray
Salon Strategies Limited

The Business Development Centre
7-15 Greatorex Street, London E1 5NF
t: +44 (0) 20 7377 9922   f: +44 (0) 20 7377 9933
anne@salonstrategies.net

www.salonstrategies.net

Working for England's World Class Region

RASHID BASHIR MBA MPhil
Head of Policy & Economics

South East England Development Agency (SEEDA)
SEEDA Headquarters Cross Lanes Guildford GU1 1YA England
Tel +44 (0)1483 500 719 **Fax** +44 (0)1483 484 247
Mobile +44 (0)7789 652784
email rashidbashir@seeda.co.uk **web** www.seeda.co.uk

 Ron Dunham

The Prince's Trust
President HRH The Prince of Wales

Room 355, Sessions House
County Road
Maidstone
Kent
ME14 1XQ

Telephone 01622 694323
Facsimile 01622 694143
ron.dunham@princes-trust.org.uk
Mobile 07703 541178
www.princes-trust.org.uk

Kanya King MBE
Founder & CEO

MOBO Organisation Ltd.
22 Stephenson Way
London NW1 2HD

T: +44 (0) 20 7419 1800
F: +44 (0) 20 7419 1600
E: kanya@mobo.com

www.mobo.com

**Royal Berkshire
Fire & Rescue Service**

MIKE PATEMAN
FIRE SAFETY INSPECTING OFFICER

Maidenhead Office, Bridge Road, Maidenhead SL6 8PG
Tel (0118) 932 2485 Fax (01628) 773193
Email patemanm@rbfrs.co.uk
www.rbfrs.co.uk

BOROUGH COUNCIL

Shabnam Ali
Learning & Economic Development Officer

Assistant Chief Executives Office
Town Hall • Bath Road • Slough • Berks • SL1 3UQ
Telephone: (01753) 875849 • Minicom No: 875030
Email: shabnam.ali@slough.gov.uk

Dr Eve Abe
Wildlife Consultant
Technical Support Team
Great Ape Survival Project

22 Verney Road Langley
Slough SL3 8NX UK
Tel: +44 (0) 1753 583715
Mob: +44 (0) 7984 307917
Born Free Office: +44 (0) 1403 240170
lawino_abe@hotmail.com
www.unep.org/grasp
www.bornfree.org.uk
charity no: 1070906

keep wildlife in the wild

Elaine Griffiths
Project Director
Mobile: +44 (0)7939 512950
Tel: +44 (0)1565 723838

The Monastery of St Francis & Gorton Trust Ltd,
3 Assisi Gardens, Gorton, Manchester. M12 5AS
Tel: +44 (0)161 223 3211.
Email: elaine@theangelsmanchester.com
www.gortonmonastery.co.uk

Mary Glomé
BSc (Hons), MCIEH

**Principal Environmental
Health Officer**

Tel : (0118) 974 6355
Fax: (0118) 974 6401
Email: mary.glome@wokingham.gov.uk

Planning, Regulation & Enforcement Service
P.O. Box 155, Shute End
Wokingham, Berkshire RG40 1WR

Wokingham District Council - A Unitary Authority
www.wokingham.gov.uk

Service Management Consultants

PO Box 1202
Maidenhead
Berkshire SL6 5YD

tel/fax: +44 (0)1628 780808
mobile: 0973 241308
email: drgwhyte@aol.com
website: www.SMF-Method.com

Dr. Grafton Whyte PhD
Research Director

---

icreation
connecting brands to people

Kofi Debrah

icreation Limited
42 Roth Walk
Durham Road
London
N7 7RJ
United Kingdom

tel +44 (0) 20 7272 2709
mob +44 (0) 7866 362 343

email: kofi@icreation.info
web: www.icreation.info

The ZAHID MUBAREK INQUIRY

Bruce Gill
Inquiry Secretary
Inquiry Team

P O Box 38560
London SW1H 9WA
Telephone 020 7936 9502
Fax 020 7936 9119
Email bruce.gill@mubarekinquiry.gsi.gov.uk
www.zahidmubarekinquiry.org.uk

The Technology Centre
Bridging the Skills Gap

Dr Ken Ife
BSc PhD, MBA, LLM, D.Eng, FRSM, MBAE

Unit A2, N17 Studios, 784 High Road, London N17 0DA.
Tel: 020 8376 8464, Fax: 020 8806 6575 Mob: 07956 382 977
41 Market Square, Edmonton, London N9 0TZ
Tel: 020 8350 5678 Fax: 020 8350 5678
E-mail: kenife@aol.com Web Site: www.techo-centre.com

Patrick Shine
Development Manager

UnLtd*

UnLtd
123 Whitecross Street
Islington
London
EC1Y 8JJ

Telephone
020 7566 1126
Fax
020 7566 1101
Email
patrickshine@unltd.org.uk
Website
www.unltd.org.uk

---

theterrace

Patrick Williams
Director

Lincoln's Inn Fields London WC2A 3LJ
T. +44 (0) 20 7430 1234 F. +44 (0) 20 7430 1154
chef7@btinternet.com www.theterrace.info

Thames Valley University
Faculty of Health & Human Sciences
32 - 38 Uxbridge Road
Ealing London W5 2BS
Telephone: +44 (0) 20 8280 5109
Facsimile: +44 (0) 20 8280 5125
E-mail: elizabeth.anionwu@tvu.ac.uk
Website: http://www.maryseacole.com

TVU
LONDON

Professor Elizabeth Anionwu RN HV Tutor PhD CBE
Head of the Mary Seacole Centre for Nursing Practice

Index

Where surnames have not been stated in the text, individuals are indexed by their forename.

accountants 16, 77, 130, 152
accounts
    see also income
    banking 129, 130, 151–2, 179
    invoices 129–30, 152
    payments 152, 177–9, 179–81
advertisement see marketing
advertising agencies 209
Alfred 22–3
Andrew 22–3
Apollo Karate Club, Reading 60
Apollo Youth Club, Reading 225, 226
appearance 71, 93
appraisals 70, 117
apprenticeships 43
arbitration 178
Arts Council 103
autobiographies 192

bank accounts 129, 130, 151–2, 179
bank loans 134–5

bank transfers 130, 152, 180
bed and breakfast 75, 79, 85–6
benefits, unemployment 49–51, 79
Berkshire County Council 44, 222
Big Debate, The 111, 112–13
Black, Asian, and Minority Ethnic (BAME) communities 97–8, 139–40, 141, 222
boxing 59–60, 61–2
Bramshill Police Training College 99
Buckinghamshire University 190
business cards 128, 208, 244
Business Link 140–1, 142
business management course 190
business plans 28, 51, 67–8, 69, 80–81, 133, 135
business premises 145–7
buyouts 82–3

café management 195–9
Capital Direct 93–5
car financing 93–5, 246
card payments 152, 179–80
care industry 81–82, 115–18
Care Quality Commission (CQC) 115, 116, 117, 118
cash payments 152, 180–81
CCL Financial Services 91, 93
charitable projects 213, 216, 226, 229
  see also community projects
  InBiz 214–15
  Next Step 213–15
  Reading Refocus 88
Charities Commission 192
cheques 129, 152, 179
Christie, Linford 22
commission 91–2, 94, 95, 180
communication 160–61, 178
  see also marketing
community projects 85–8, 106, 160, 215–16
  see also charitable projects
  The Big Debate 111, 112–13
  MAP Partnership Community Centre 225–9
  Urban News 103–7

competition 23–4, 28, 141, 153, 170–71, 173
confrontation 98
contracts 99, 178
County Court Judgements (CCJs) 151
court action 178
crime 16, 44–5
criticism 121–5, 165–6
  constructive criticism 122
customer service 92, 152, 154, 160–61
  during disputes 177–8

debts 151–2
Devana Care 246, 256
diaries 154
Disclosure and Barring Service (DBS) 116
disputes 177–8
diversification 172–4

economic downturn 79–80
electronic bank transfers 130, 152, 180
email 127, 154, 157, 207
employees 70, 116, 117, 118, 197, 203
  interviewing 47, 50, 54, 68–9, 86, 116–17
  managers and team leaders 82, 86, 116, 219–21
  recruitment 115, 116–17, 201, 203
employment see self-employment
employment legislation 4, 202

Equalities and Human
    Rights Commission
    (EHRC) 97
equipment, for businesses
    153
events organisation 214

Facebook 207, 209–10
financial advice 91–3, 130,
    173
financial brokerage 93–5
fitness 63–4
freelance work 99, 239
Freestyle (band) 37, 38
Frogs and Trogs 27–9

get-rich-quick schemes 16,
    56
goals 2, 71, 219
grants 136
Groveland's Primary School,
    Reading 9

Hamilton House, Berkshire
    81, 82–3
Harrogate Police Training
    College 99
health 63–4, 70
health and safety
    requirements 71, 154
health and social care
    industry 81–82,
    115–18
Henley-on-Thames 145–6
Hexagon, Reading 37
hire purchase agreements 94
HM Revenue and Customs
    (HMRC) 140

holiday pay 70
Home Office 97
home working 70
hospitality industry 195–9,
    214
Human League, The 37

InBiz 214–15
income 2, 76, 77, 128, 136,
    209
Instagram 210
insurance 91, 92, 95, 153,
    154, 173
internet presence 140,
    154–5, 207
    email 127, 154, 157, 207
    social media 157, 158,
        207–11
    websites 128–9, 152, 159,
        171, 208,
        209
interviews, job 47, 50, 54,
    68–9, 86, 116–17
invoices 129–30, 152
    see also accountants;
        payments

Jamaica 231–5
James ('Sugar Browne') 27,
    29
Jimmy 87
Job Centre 151
Joe 221–2

karate 60–61
Kensington 74–5
Khartoum, Sudan 34–5

Knowledge Centre, London
141

Langley, Berkshire 49
leadership 2–4
leaflets 93, 128, 157
legal advice 151, 152, 154,
177
Lemon Hall, Jamaica 231–5
lesbian, gay, bisexual, and
transgender
(LGBTQ)
communities 98
licences 3–4, 152, 154, 178
limited companies 152
LinkedIn 211
loans 15, 80, 134–5
see also mortgages
local authorities 86, 110,
112, 115, 116, 196

Mac 85
magazine advertisements
158
magazines 87
Today Magazine 107
trade magazines 154, 159
Urban News 103–7
Magnolia Lodge, Reading
81, 82–3
Maidenhead 75
management 2–3, 117,
201–4
business management
course 190
delegation of 82, 86, 116,
219–21
self-appraisal 70
tour (bands) 35–6, 37

Mandela, Nelson 104
MAP Partnership 225–9
market research 127–31,
140
marketing 116, 128, 157–8,
173
see also communication
methods 93, 112, 158–9
business cards 128,
208, 244
leaflets 93, 128, 157
social media 207–11
plans 68, 80
Mars (confectionary) 13,
47–9
martial arts 60–62
Mary Seacole Day Nursery,
Reading 225, 226
maternity leave 69
Mayfield, Curtis 37
Meadway Secondary
School, Reading 9,
14, 19–20, 41–2
meetings 134, 202
mentors 85–8, 103, 221–2
Merton Technical College,
London 43
Michael ('Mick') 27, 29, 37,
38
mindset 14–15, 16
minimum wage 118
minority groups 97–8, 110,
139–41, 222, 241
mission statements 133,
240–41
Mobay Autos 246
mobile phone industry
145–8

mortgages 73, 76–7, 91, 92
motor neurone disease
    (MND) 255–7

negativity 121–5, 165–6
Nesta Care 115–16
networking 16
  see also social media
newspaper advertisements
    93, 157, 158, 208
Next Step 213–15
Notting Hill Carnival 36–7

office space 70, 93

parental leave 68–9
partnerships 219–21
  see also MAP Partnership
pay 2, 76, 77, 128, 136, 209
payments 152, 177–9,
    179–81
  see also invoices
pension plans 54–5, 92, 118
PHAB, Berkshire 225, 226
Pinterest 211
policing 97–101
premises 145–7
pricing 127, 169–72
promotion *see* marketing
property investment 73–7,
    79–80, 81–3, 85–6
  see also premises
qualifications 22, 42, 73,
    190–91

radio advertisements 158,
    208
Reading Amateur Boxing
    Club 59

Reading, Berkshire
  Cemetery Junction 22
  Groveland's Primary
    School 9
  Groveland's Road 10
  MAP Partnership
    Community Centre
    225
  Meadway Secondary
    School 9, 14, 19–20,
    41–2
Reading Community
    Carnival 103
Reading Education and
    Business Partnership
    86
Reading Refocus 88
recruitment 115, 116–17,
    201, 203
  see also interviews, job
Redingensians Rugby Club
    62
reggae music 33–7
responsibility 183–7
restaurant management
    195–9
retail industry 145–9
reviews, customer 171
risk assessments 154
risk taking 163–4
role models 85–8, 103,
    221–2
rugby 62–3

self-appraisal 70
self-employment 2–3, 5, 91,
    121
  failure of businesses
    123–4

financing of 15, 80,
134–5, 251
flexibility of 64, 198–9,
217
freelance work 99, 239
income 2, 76, 77, 128,
136, 209
rules and regulations 3–4,
91, 94
starting a business 55,
128–9, 135–6
business plans 28, 51,
67–8, 69, 80–81,
133, 135
mission statements 133,
240–41
'sole trader' 151–5, 157
support for 130, 140–41
accountants 16, 77,
130, 152
legal advice 151, 152,
154, 177
self-help books 16, 155,
192–3, 251–2
Seville, Keith 6, 27, *108*,
261–2
birth and childhood 7,
8–9, 10, 13–14, 19
charitable and community
projects 106, 160
The Big Debate 111,
112–13
InBiz 214–15
MAP Partnership
Community Centre
225–9
mentoring scheme 86–7
Next Step 213–15
Reading Refocus 88

Urban News 103–7
education 9–10, 19, 22–4,
42, 43, 190–91
employment 4–5, 30, 33–7,
41–3, 53
Court Welfare Officer
44–5
CCL Financial Services
91, 93
Mars factory 47–9
paper round 13, 29–31
family 7–8, 9–10, 13, 30,
48, 258
Jamaican roots 231–5
working with 74, 81–3
self-employment 246
café management 195–9
care homes 81–82,
115–18
financial advice and
brokerage 91–5
Frogs and Trogs 27–9
magazine publishing
103–7
mobile phone retail
145–8
police training 99–101
property investment
73–7, 79–80, 81–3,
85–6
sporting ability 19–22,
59–62
Seville, Monica 8, 255–9
Seville, Paulette 8
Seville Care Homes 81, 82
Seville Lodge, Wokingham
81, 82
shops 145–7
sick leave 70, 202

Slough, Berkshire 47, 48, 49, 141
Slough Leadership Challenge 140
Snapchat 208, 209
Social Enterprise Berkshire 215–16
social media 157, 158, 207–11
'sole traders' 151, 152, 157–8
solicitors 16, 44, 152, 178
staff *see* employees
Stonehenge Festival 37
sub-contracting 99
Sulhampstead Police Training College 99
'supported living' 115
surveys 127

'Take Six Boys' 28
teaching 190–91
team leaders 219
teamwork 59, 246
Thames Valley University 190
Tilehurst, Reading 22
Timmy 22–3
Today Magazine 107
Tokyo, Japan 35–6
trade magazines 154, 159
training courses 91, 92, 192–3, 202, 213
    business management 190–91, 202
    carers 82, 115
    in policing 97–101
Twitter 210

unemployment 14, 56, 95, 184
    benefits 49–51, 79
    charities 213, 214
    'unemployability' 53–4, 56
university post-graduate courses 190–91
Urban Aid 44
Urban News 103–7
Urban UK Network 109–10
Urban Warrior (band) 33–7

vehicles, business 154
verbal agreements 178
voluntary community projects 85–8, 106, 160, 215–16
    see also charitable projects
    The Big Debate 111, 112–13
    MAP Partnership Community Centre 225–9
    Urban News 103–7

websites 128–9, 152, 159, 171, 208, 209
    social media 157, 158, 207–11
Welch 37, 38, 109
WhatsApp 157, 208
women, in business 142–3
written agreements *see* contracts

YouTube 158, 209